THE GAME OF THREE HALVES AND OTHER BIZARRE FOOTBALL STORIES

To the footballers of my childhood who didn't wear earrings, gloves or tights but turned out in freezing temperatures in short-sleeved shirts and kicked and headed a saturated ball that felt like a ton.

First published by Carlton Books in 2010 as *1001 Bizarre Football Stories*.

This updated edition published in 2012.

Carlton Books
20 Mortimer Street
London W1T 3JW

1001bizarrestories.com

Editorial: Jo Murray, Bronagh Woods and Barry Goodman

A CIP catalogue for this book is available from the British Library.

ISBN 978-1-78097-200-8

Printed and bound by CPI Group (UK) Ltd, Croydon, CR0 4YY

Other hilarious titles from Carlton Books include:
The Dog that Survived the Titanic and Other Amazing Animal Stories
Opening his Legs and Showing his Class: The Funniest and Daftest Sports Commentary Ever
The Big Book of Football's Funniest Quotes
Being the Gaffer! The Crazy World of the Football Manager

THE GAME OF THREE HALVES

AND OTHER BIZARRE FOOTBALL STORIES

Robert Lodge

CARLTON
BOOKS

Robert Lodge has spent a working lifetime with words as a journalist and author. Although his knowledge of sport is extensive, his great love is the game of football with all its faults, foibles and idiosyncrasies and he has covered the sport for a number of influential publications. His previous books include *1001 Greatest Football Moments*, *The Little Book of West Ham* and *The Dog that Survived the Titanic and Other Amazing Animal Stories*.

INTRODUCTION

Football, one of the most enduring games and arguably now the biggest money-spinning sport on the planet, has attracted every type of character in its 150 years of organized history. Out of all the players, coaches, referees, directors or owners, there have been a select few passing through football history who have added some extra-special spice and zest and have made the headlines as a result – often not always to the benefit of the sport's image.

In compiling the book I have been astounded by the follies, saddened by the tragedies and laughed at the ridiculous. Picking the highlights from so many bizarre and strange happenings is difficult but in what other sport would a chairman propose a crocodile-filled moat around the pitch to stop troublesome crowd invasions? What are the odds of a passing seagull being blasted out of the sky by a goalkeeper's high kick or angry fans laying into each other – with sticks of celery?

The Game of Three Halves and Other Bizarre Football Stories is not just about the bad boys – and girls – who have besmirched the good name of the game; it is a celebration of the quirkiness that makes the game so much richer.

Robert Lodge, 2012

Bomb surprise after 50 years

Thousands of players spanning half a century found that they had been playing on a time bomb. In April 1995 a half-ton German bomb was discovered under a football pitch that had been the venue for thousands of amateur games over more than 50 years. Rendering the monster bomb from World War 2 safe meant mounting, up until that time, Britain's biggest peacetime bomb disposal operation. It meant that the 4,000 inhabitants of the Isle of Portland in Dorset had to be evacuated as army bomb disposal teams moved in. The bomb was defused after hours of tense work.

Kidnapped team murdered

Mystery still surrounds the murders of ten amateur players who were kidnapped in Venezuela in 2009. They were members of a team, most of them Colombians, taken by armed men who called out their names one by one. Of the 12, ten were found murdered execution-style, one was found alive and another remained unaccounted for. The single survivor, 19-year-old Manuel Cortez, said he was forced to his knees and shot in the neck. He told police the team were held alive for 14 days before the systematic murders began.

Nice rice

Nineteenth-century England goalkeeper Jack Robinson was so superstitious he reckoned eating a plate of rice pudding before a match brought him luck. On one occasion when he couldn't get the milk pudding he conceded 11 goals.

New boss names names

A new manager taking over is an insecure time for players who might not fit into his plans, but when Gordon Strachan took over at Middlesbrough in 2009 some of his squad were in for a shock. At his initial press conference he held a piece of paper that looked like his ideal team sheet and, worryingly for the then-current squad, eight of the 12 names on the list were prospective signings. While star names of the squad such as Brad Jones, David Wheater, Sean St Ledger or Adam Johnson were there, so were his targets who he thought would best make a promotion challenge back to the Premier League. The list hardly inspired confidence for the 24 Boro squad members.

Splinter kills player

A player died after a splinter punctured his intestine during an indoor game in Rio de Janiero, Brazil. The player was making a tackle in the 2010 game when the splinter broke off from the wooden floor.

Wanted "villains" were actors

In one of the most bizarre police mix-ups, the photographs of actors from a hit film were issued to the media as "Wanted" football hooligans after a riot by London football fans. Scotland Yard apologised in 2009 for the mistake in issuing 66 pictures of people supposedly caught on camera during violent clashes between West Ham and Millwall fans. The images wrongly included stills of six actors from a recent film The Firm. The Metropolitan Police explained that a TV report was used to capture the images but because there was no sound officers did not realise it included clips from the hooligan-themed film.

The taxman cometh for Maradona

Every return trip to Italy after his playing days there seemed to cost Argentinian maestro Diego Maradona money. In September 2009 his return sparked a police raid on the health clinic where he was staying to recover another tranche of unpaid taxes. Maradona had to hand over a diamond earring, as part-payment of an alleged tax bill from his time at Napoli from 1984 to 1991. It later fetched €25,000 at auction. Ironically Maradona was said to be at the clinic for stress treatment. On a previous visit to Naples in 2006 police had pounced to take two Rolex watches worth an estimated €10,000.

Coin clash

Liverpool's Jamie Carragher was so furious at being struck by a £1 coin thrown from the crowd in an FA Cup tie with Arsenal in 2002 – he angrily threw it back. It cost the defender a red card, a £40,000 club fine and a temporary loss of his England place.

High Roller

Saeed Owairan scored the deciding goal against Belgium that saw Saudi Arabia qualify from the group stage of the World Cup 1994 and received a new Rolls-Royce.

Serial offender

Bulgarian referee Angel Angelou was suspended in 2010 for the third time in three years. The Bulgarian Football Union said he had favoured Levski Sofia with a penalty decision. He had previously been banned for bias towards another club from the capital Sofia, CSKA.

Total wipeout for Rooney

Many rival players have tried to wipe out England star Wayne Rooney on the pitch – and failed. Not so the monkeys at two wildlife parks which have vandalized the Manchester United striker's car on two occasions. While visiting a safari park in the north of England in 2012 a monkey ripped off a rear windscreen wiper and ran away with it. It was déjà vu for hotshot Rooney and his son Kai for the same thing had happened to them at another wildlife park in 2011.

Maradona's on target – with a gun

Former Argentine star Diego Maradona did what many celebrities relentlessly pursued by journalists and the paparazzi may have wanted to do but didn't dare – he hit back. But Maradona did it with an air rifle. In the 1994 incident outside Maradona's Buenos Aires home, four people were injured. TV footage showed Maradona, who was found guilty of assault with a weapon, crouched behind a car with two other men firing an air gun at reporters.

Small fry fried

When a cash-strapped Premier League needed to slash costs, £60-a-day ground staff were axed while a £10,000-a-week senior executive was retained, although he had agreed to a pay cut.

Only in America

The USA introduced electronic golf-style buggies for the 1994 World Cup. They were used to transport injured players from the field but their use was lambasted for slowing the game down.

Ref joins the gunners

Shooting on target took on a different meaning in South Africa in 1999. During a pitch invasion by home fans of Hartbeesfontein Wallabies caused by Try Agains cutting their lead to 2–1, a Wallabies' player left the field and returned with a knife. Witnesses said he lunged at the referee who had meanwhile armed himself with a 9mm pistol from a friend in the crowd and shot the player in the chest. The ref, whose gun was said to be licensed, denied causing the player's death. Later it was revealed the cause of the unrest was believed to be heavy unlicensed betting on the game.

Roared off

Macclesfield mascot, Roary the Lion, was red-carded for making obscene gestures during a players' brawl in a 1998 match with Lincoln City.

Chickened out

A Manchester City fan was banned in 1995 from bringing dead chickens into the ground. Club authorities objected to him swinging the birds around his head whenever City scored.

Nutty Brazil

Brazil launched a system of IQ and psychological profiling for potential squad members. Legendary Garrincha, famous for his mercurial dribbling, failed both but starred in Brazil's 1958 and 1962 World Cup wins.

Ronaldo sidesteps serious injury

Roadside barriers did a better job of stopping Cristiano Ronaldo than many international defenders had when he crashed his £200,000 Ferrari in 2008. During his time playing for Manchester United, the Portuguese winger who is famous for his stepovers, escaped unhurt after crashing his high-powered sports car into a tunnel barrier. He emerged from the car to survey the vehicle, which had serious body damage and a sheared-off front wheel. The Ferrari 599 GTB was just one of a fleet of prestige cars owned by the player who later moved to Real Madrid for a world record fee.

Late-comer

A former first division manager revealed that at one of his clubs players had a sweepstake on who could have sex closest to a 3pm kick-off. The winner clocked 2.55pm.

Police pepper players

Riot police stormed on to the pitch and pepper-sprayed players after a row over a red card during a 2010 match in Brazil. A player in a Rondionese League game between Genus and Moto Clube refused to walk after being dismissed and police in full riot gear charged him and his protesting team-mates. The match was abandoned but an investigation into the police actions was launched.

Death mob

A disgruntled mob killed Benin's under-20 international goalkeeper Yessoufo Samiou after they attacked him following a bad result. He died from neck and arm injuries after Benin lost 3-0 to Nigeria in the 2005 African Youth Championship.

Weedy excuse

A gardening accident left a goalkeeper's career in the balance in 2008. Antigua's Janiel Simon damaged his right eye with a weed whacker and needed urgent surgery.

Marseille's tarnished crown

The euphoria of winning the European Champions' League masked the sham behind Marseille's 1993 triumph. Crowned France's first European champions with a shock win over AC Milan, it soon emerged Marseille had no right to be in the final. It was discovered their president had bribed French club Valenciennes into throwing a league game that allowed Marseille to win the French league – giving them more time to concentrate on the upcoming European final. Marseille were stripped of their title and barred from defending their European crown as a result.

Virgin on ridiculous

In a 2010 poll Tottenham Hotspur's 6ft 7ins striker Peter Crouch was voted the funniest man in British sport for his one-liners. When asked what he would have been if he were not a star player, he replied: "a virgin!".

Match led to war and 6,000 deaths

Stones thrown at the hotel windows of the El Salvador national team sparked a war that left 6,000 dead, 15,000 injured and thousands homeless. The stoning plan by Honduran fans to disturb the El Salvador team's sleep before a 1969 fixture spiralled out of control. The El Salvadorans lost 1–0 and a woman fan shot herself in despair. When the teams met later in San Salvador several Hondurans were killed in revenge for Amelia Bolanios' death. The ensuing 100-hours' war between the two countries brought horror to thousands.

Game of three halves

An 1894 English league game was unique for having three halves. The Sunderland-Derby County match started with a deputising referee and played 45 minutes. When the delayed ref finally turned up he ordered a full 90-minute game played. Over the 135 minutes Sunderland scored 11 goals without reply.

Brawl boys

Bad boy players are never safe from the wrath of the referee – even in the dressing room. A March 2012 match in League Two produced a record of which no one was proud. Five players were sent off – after the final whistle had gone. The mass dismissal in the dressing rooms followed a post-match brawl that disfigured Crawley Town's 2-1 win at Bradford. Three home players – Andrew Davies, Luke Oliver and the goalkeeper Jon McLaughlin – were given red cards by referee Iain Williamson, who also sent off the Crawley pair Kyle McFadzean and Claude Davis. Six Crawley players and one from Bradford had earlier been booked during an already ill-tempered match. Club fines and FA suspensions followed for the battling protagonists. Later Crawley skipper Pablo Mills was stripped of the club captaincy for his part in the brawl.

What a Pratt!

David Pratt had been on the field just three seconds before he got a red card for his first action of the game between non-league Chippenham Town and Bashley in England in 2008.

Naked aggression

Adrian Bastia's tackling of a streaker in 2008 earned him a red card. The Greek player went after the naked invader during his side Asteras Tripolis' game with Panathinaikos and tripped him, sending the invader sprawling.

Lightning sparks witchcraft fears

Black magic conspiracy theories came to the fore when lightning wiped out a complete team but spared their opponents in a match staged in the Democratic Republic of Congo. The lightning bolt killed 11 players aged between 20 and 35 from the Bena Tshadi team, who were drawing 1–1 at home with visitors Basangana. Although 30 other people were treated for burns, the only deaths were from Bena Tshadi and that began rumblings among those in this region of the world who fear witchcraft and where fetishes are widely used in football. The match was abandoned.

Bird strike

Tomas Brolin missed the start of pre-season training at Leeds United after a bird hit his car windscreen and caused him to miss his flight from Sweden to England.

Festival gaffe

Goalkeeper Jens Lehmann was dropped from Stuttgart's first-team squad during 2009 when he was spotted at Munich's beer festival without permission just hours after his side had been beaten 2–0 by Cologne.

Thomas forges a new career

Welsh international Mickey Thomas didn't shrink from the limelight after serving 18 months in prison for forgery in 1993. After being freed from jail, the former Manchester United midfielder made his crime of printing £10 notes and distributing them the focus of his performances on the lucrative after-dinner speaking circuit. Among his quips was: "Roy Keane [a Manchester United star of the time] is on £50,000 a week. So was I until the police found my printing machine." Much-travelled Thomas played for 11 clubs in England, Wales and the USA during a 21-year playing career and was capped 51 times for his country.

Plucky player

David Beckham was outed by his wife as a man who plucks his eyebrows. Victoria Beckham let the girly secret slip during a promotional tour of Japan in 2003.

Generous George

Star player George Weah paid for his team-mates' uniforms and expenses so that Liberia could enter the 1996 Africa Cup of Nations in South Africa. They finished bottom of their group.

Bloodshed was pre-match fare

Forget mascots and scantily clad cheerleaders for the pre-match entertainment during the Taliban rule of Afghanistan in the 1990s. Cold-blooded murder was on view before matches at Kabul's main soccer stadium. There were huge attendances to see men and women, who had fallen foul of the harsh Taliban rule, shot, have their throats cut or have limbs amputated – and all before the teams took the field. The stadium was often packed with men and women, many of whom had brought their children, who chanted "God is great" as the executions were carried out.

Clarke's game for TV

Burnley defender Clarke Carlisle became the first Premier League player to win in the popular British TV series *Countdown* which is considered more cerebral than average quizzes. In tribute at the next Burnley home match in 2010 Carlisle's name was made into an anagram in the programme team list.

Sizzling price for a player

It is not known if Romanian league player Marius Cioara had promised to "skin" attacking forwards but the price of his transfer from UT Arad to Regal Hornia in 2006 was 15 kilos of pork sausages. However, the move was not a happy one as it lasted only a day. Fed up with sausage-related ribbing from his new team-mates, he quit to work on a farm in Spain, saying he was hugely insulted. It left Regal Hornia demanding back their fee – a day's worth of team dinners – from UT Arad.

Smart turn-out

Referee Jean Langenus of Belgium wore a suit jacket, golfing plus fours and a red striped tie when he officiated at the 1930 World Cup final in Uruguay.

Tweeting twit?

Football fans on Twitter sprang into fevered action when Joleon Lescott mentioned on the social network that he had a cold and was about to take a Lemsip to reduce the symptoms. In his April 2012 tweet the Manchester City centre-back seemed unaware that the popular cold remedy contains substances on the FIFA banned list and that taking the medicine might get him a suspension for using stimulants. The Twittersphere lit up and his employers rapidly contacted the player to stop him taking the remedy. Fortunately, the England international had not actually got around to doing it yet.

Loose talk costs England career

Maverick Rodney Marsh's slick footwork was legendary but his equally slick tongue killed a burgeoning England international career in 1973 after just nine caps. England manager, Alf Ramsey, already wary of Marsh's reputation for fading in and out of the action, told him: 'I'll be watching you for the first 45 minutes and if you don't work harder I'll pull you off at half-time." Marsh's retort, "Crikey, Alf, at Manchester City [Marsh's club] all we get is an orange and a cup of tea," was greeted with stony silence – he was never selected for England again.

Critic dies

There was outrage when killer footballer Javier Florez was freed from prison on £45,000 bail. Colombian Florez was jailed in 2009 after shooting dead a fan who annoyed him. He said: "I was drunk. He really upset me."

Putting snap into crowd control

A moat filled with crocodiles was the crazy idea for curbing pitch invasions at the Steaua Nicolae Balcescu club in Romania. Faced with expulsion because of repeated pitch invasions by his volatile fans, club chairman Alexandra Cringus needed a plan. In a bizarre light bulb moment he proposed a moat full of crocs around the pitch. He even had the welfare of players and crocodiles sorted. The moat would be far enough away from the pitch to stop players falling in and the reptilian residents would have heated water in the winter and meat from the local slaughterhouse.

High-priced gardener

£20,000-a-week winger Gabriel Obertan pruned rose bushes at Manchester United's training ground while recovering from a back injury in 2009.

Beer incentive

A brewery's offer of a lifetime's supply of free beer to the first Austrian to score in the Euro 2008 tournament did not produce an avalanche of goals. Ivica Vastic won the prize by notching the country's only goal of the competition – a 93rd-minute penalty.

Penalty penalty

Two men pleaded guilty to stealing the penalty spots from the Rotherham ground as a Christmas prank. They broke into the ground and dug up the spots.

Unsuitable viewing

Bruce Rioch first knew about his sacking as Queen's Park Rangers assistant manager by reading about it on British TV information service Ceefax in November 1997.

The face of revenge

Toilet humour was lost on the management team of Brazil's international side when axed striker Romario made revenge an art form. Romario, famous for his humour and his clashes with authority, had cartoons of national manager Mario Zagallo and his assistant Zico painted on the toilet doors of the sports bar he owns in Rio de Janeiro. Zagallo was depicted sitting on the toilet, while Zico was drawn with a loo roll in his hand. Furious Zagallo, not famed for his sense of humour, took the issue to court and won. As a result, Romario was ordered to remove the offending doors and pay damages.

A bunch of stand-up guys

A team physiotherapist admitted in 2009 that the erectile dysfunction medication, Viagra, was given to players in Bolivia. Blooming, a team that plays at sea level, were trying to overcome the disadvantage of playing opposition from the Altiplano, which is at over 4,000 metres. Viagra works by opening blood vessels so that oxygen is absorbed more efficiently. There had been strong denials about the practice until Blooming's physio admitted it. The World Anti-Doping Agency was conducting clinical trials to see whether Viagra should be listed as a banned substance.

Sitting comfortably?

Estudiantes coach Carlos Bilardo moved a deckchair, patio table, radio and champagne to the touchline for his side's 2004 clash with River Plate. He explained he wanted to enjoy the spectacle, but unfortunately his team didn't provide one, losing 3–0.

Wedding day arrest

Australian goalkeeper Mark Bosnich was arrested outside a strip club on the morning of his wedding.

Boy, what a debut?

Bolivian Mauricio Baldivieso, aged just 12, became the youngest debutant in South American senior football when he played nine minutes as a substitute in Aurora's 1–0 defeat to La Paz. The boy's father, Aurora coach and Bolivian 1994 World Cup midfielder Julio Cesar Baldivieso, had to watch impotently from the stands as La Paz players dealt out some rough footballing lessons that left the boy in tears. Peruvian Fernando Garcia, 13 in 2001, had been the previous youngest.

Good neighbours

Luxury homes were built in Bucharest for Romania's top players to live near each other. Those who bought into "Footballers' Street" included internationals Cosmin Contra and Adrian Mutu.

Keeper's "other" white lines

Colombian international goalkeeper Rene Higuita tested positive for cocaine in 2004 while playing for an Ecuadorian club – the second time drug associations have wrecked his career. Flamboyant Higuita was imprisoned in 1993, over a drug-related kidnapping. Acting as a go-between for two drug barons, he was largely responsible for securing the release of a young woman by delivering the ransom money. The $64,000 he received broke a Colombian law on profiting from kidnapping. In jail for seven months before being released without charge meant Higuita was not fit for the 1994 World Cup.

Thieves score

The north-west of England has not always been the best place for footballers to settle. Audacious thieves have targeted a dozen stars' homes often while the victims have been away playing or training. Among the high-profile victims have been Liverpool players Jermaine Pennant, Jerzy Dudek, Pepe Reina, Lucas Leiva and Peter Crouch, and Andy van der Meyde of Everton. The thieves' swag included an Olympic bronze medal, cars, TVs, jewellery and watches – even a puppy. Police recovered many items because club fans, angry at the treatment of their heroes, rang the cops with vital information.

Baby in a hurry

Everton goalkeeper Richard Wright and wife Kelly had the birth of their first baby Bo induced to ensure the player could turn out for a major game.

It's murder for frightened ref

A referee who thought he was under threat after awarding a yellow card, ended up shooting one man and injuring two others. In an incident during a match in 2004 coach Michael Sizani and players of the Marselle side playing the Mighty Elevens in the Eastern Cape district of South Africa advanced to protest, but ref Ncedisile Zakhe pulled a pistol and killed Sizani. Opposition coach Mbuzeli Ziqula and Mighty Eleven player Zandisile George were hit in the hands by the same bullet. The ref fled the scene but was eventually caught and subsequently spent four years behind bars for culpable homicide and other offences.

What a sauce!

Diego Simeone berated his Argentinian team-mates to be more manly after they celebrated goals with "The Ketchup Song" dance in 2002.

Thieves slam Dunc-ed

A thief reckoned without the fearsome reputation of Everton striker Duncan Ferguson in 2001. Fiery Ferguson caught a burglar trying to make off with CDs and champagne from the Scottish international's home near Liverpool. "Big Dunc" – he is 6 feet 4 inches – sat on him until police arrived. But still the underworld didn't learn because two years later another burglar Ferguson caught in the act needed hospital treatment. The raider tried to press an assault charge against Ferguson, failed and got himself a four-year prison sentence into the bargain.

Prank goes sour

Two former England footballers were arrested in London in July 2007 when they were found with a limousine reported stolen. Former Newcastle United team-mates Rob Lee and Warren Barton were found at addresses close to an allegedly stolen Mercedes E220 saloon that had been involved in a collision with a van. No charges were made by the police and midfielders Lee and Barton – who had retired from the game several years before – dismissed the incident as a prank, involving others.

Bursting in

An England fan looking for loo accidently invaded the national team's dressing room after their disappointing 2010 World Cup draw with Algeria.

Pitch invasion – by cops

A drug dealer on the run from jail was recaptured as he played in a Sunday league match in Leeds, England, in 2009. Twenty police interrupted the match to arrest the man – but his team still won 6–3.

Game goes down the drain

A pass out to the wing in a boys' school match went astray – because the intended recipient had disappeared from sight. The 4-year-old winger fell down a manhole during the 2012 game at Daniel James Community School in Swansea. One minute Tom Halfpenny was in the game, the next he was wedged down the previously unseen manhole and calling for help. The brave boy was swiftly pulled out and a medical check revealed him surprised but unhurt after the incident.

Winner becomes three-time loser

Peter Storey, a member of Arsenal's 1970–71 double-winning side, had a spectacular fall from grace after retiring. The England international defender who had won the unique double of FA Cup and English First Division winners' medals in the same season retired to a life of crime – and prison. The slide began with a £700 fine and six-month suspended jail sentence in 1979 for running a brothel and the following year he was sentenced to three years in jail after financing a plot to counterfeit gold coins. In 1990 he was behind bars again for 28 days for trying to smuggle 20 pornographic movies in the spare tyre of his car.

Match-fixing crackdown

Italian football authorities were ruthless in 2006 in crushing corruption at the highest level of its clubs. After an inquiry proving match fixing, heavy punishments were handed down. Champions Juventus were relegated and stripped of their last two Serie A titles. The additional deduction of 30 points from the following season's total, condemned Juve to at least two seasons in Serie B. Lazio and Fiorentina were also demoted and AC Milan handed a 15-point penalty. The teams were accused of rigging games by selecting favourable referees after police phone taps revealed a cosy relationship between team managers and referee organisations.

Bad break

In a 1966 English fourth division game against Aldershot both Chester full backs broke their legs and had to be carried off. Both were called Jones – Ray and Bryn – and both broke their left legs and ended up in the same hospital ward.

Whistle blown on corrupt ref

A giant-killing cup shock led to the exposure of one of the most shameful episodes in German football history and ended with referee Robert Hoyzer being jailed for 29 months. Hoyzer confessed to trying to fix matches and destroyed the feel-good factor the success of staging the 2006 World Cup had given the country. Hoyzer's favouring of underdogs Paderborn in their shock 4–2 cup win over Hamburg resulted in protests to the German FA. Enquiries uncovered a murky network of corruption linked to a Croatian gambling syndicate. Ante Sapina, the Croatian who orchestrated the match fixing, was jailed for 35 months and others received lesser punishments.

Web of deceit

Eleven key championship matches had to replayed in Brazil in 2005 after a corrupt referee attempted to influence results in the country's top division for an illegal betting website. The referee admitted favouring sides in return for a fee and was banned from football for life. The replayed results caused chaos and enabled Corinthians to become Brazilian league champions at the expense of bitter rivals Internacional, who would have taken the title had the original results stood.

Legal seesaw in corruption allegations

It took four court cases to resolve allegations that former Liverpool goalkeeper Bruce Grobbelaar took £40,000 to ensure his team lost a match in 1993. Criminal charges against Grobbelaar twice went to court with juries failing to reach a verdict. The South African-born keeper sued Britain's *The Sun* newspaper for libel in 1999 and won £85,000 damages. *The Sun* appealed and in 2001 Grobbelaar's award was reduced to £1 – and he was ordered to pay huge legal costs.

Mass bans after match-fix scandal

A 1980 match-fixing scandal involving top Italian players and leading clubs led to mass arrests and a total of 50 years of bans from football for the culprits. The so-called Totonero affair, named after the term for illegal betting, involved a syndicate attempting to tamper with Serie A and B matches. It culminated in AC Milan and Lazio being relegated, while various teams incurred points deductions. International striker Paolo Rossi's three-year ban was cut to two to allow him to play in the World Cup, where he finished as the tournament's leading scorer.

Ointment excuse

The girlfriend of an Italy-based player tried to take the blame for his failed drugs test in 2007. She claimed she forgot an ointment prescribed for the sexually-transmitted disease she suffered contained the banned substance cortisone.

Long match

A Chinese soccer fan survived a severe heart attack in 2006 after drinking heavily and staying up three days and nights to watch the World Cup. Portugal missing a goal against Angola provoked the attack.

Déjà vu, vu, vu

In three successive seasons, between 1955-58, Leeds United were drawn against Cardiff City in the third round of the English FA Cup and lost by the same score, 2-1, every time.

Players jailed in betting scandal

Vietnamese authorities launched a clean-up of football in 2005 by jailing two former footballers and six national team players. Prison sentences of up to six years were handed down for those involved in a gambling scandal. All eight were found guilty of various illegal activities including taking bribes when they colluded to win by no more than 1–0. More than 30 other players and referees were also investigated. Organised betting rings involving millions of dollars are widespread in Vietnam.

Spy claim refuted

A one-time captain of Romania refuted allegations of spying for secret police during the 1980s. Defender Gheorghe Popescu denied informing on team-mates but admitted that he was approached to work for the feared Romanian secret police – the Securitate. He said he had refused. At a press conference in 2009 as he bid to head Romania's FA, Popescu said he signed a document promising to "defend the national interests" during the regime of dictator Nicolae Ceausescu but said that was common practice for players on international duty.

Winger stars at Wes' nuptials

A natty piece of wing play was a feature of the wedding of Manchester United and England defender Wes Brown and fiancée Leanne Wassell. In a scene straight out of a Harry Potter book, an owl delivered the couple's rings. Ollie the barn owl swooped over guests at the 2009 wedding bearing the couple's rings in a velvet pouch. The ceremony was at the aptly named Peckforton Castle in Cheshire. Ollie is especially trained for the task and had delivered rings for many wedding couples.

Nightclub bans

Scottish footballers Darren McCormack and Derek Riordan were barred from a large number of nightclubs in Edinburgh – because of their brawling. The two Hibernian players were banned in 2009 from all venues in the capital city's Unight security scheme. Scotland under-21 international McCormack, 20, whose father is a professional boxing trainer, apologised after his punch-up with another nightclub reveller. Riordan, despite proclaiming his innocence, was banned for five years over a string of club bust-ups in Edinburgh.

"Friendly" mass punch-up

A pitched battle is generally not in the game plan for testimonial matches but "friendly" went out the window inside 45 minutes when West Ham United met Spain's Atletico Bilbao in London. Perhaps fittingly the 1999 testimonial match was for former Hammer Julian Dicks, who was nicknamed "The Terminator" for his no-nonsense tackling. The wild challenges came thick and fast and tempers snapped just before half-time when a ruck of mass proportions erupted. Spectators witnessed a 17-man punch-up, which resulted in Paolo di Canio being sent off and Atletico winning 2–1.

Smooth move

In 2006 Reading goalkeeper Marcus Hahnemann refused to shave his bottom lip until he conceded a goal. His unbeaten run lasted seven weeks before he reached for the razor.

Ladies, please!

A women's match between Cesmac and So Esporte left one player hospitalised in an on-field rumpus involving at least 13 players punching, kicking and hair pulling.

Dust-up wrecks relations

A practice session ended up looking like rehearsals for a Bruce Lee movie when China's Olympic team held a two-week training camp in England in 2007. One training session was hosted by west London club Queen's Park Rangers (QPR) amid which a brawl exploded involving almost every player plus coaches and bystanders. In the mayhem punches and kung-fu kicks flew and eventually seven players were sent home. China's Zheng Tao was knocked out and suffered a fractured jaw in the melee. QPR were fined £20,000.

Fight was a TV disgrace

Soccer violence can be infectious and in one televised brawl transmitted to millions even the press got involved. A Thailand–Qatar international collapsed into havoc live on TV in 1998. The spark that ended in a brawl involving all 22 players came after Qataris disputed a decision by referee Ekchai Thanatdeunkhao for more than five minutes – then Thai players got involved. The game was eventually abandoned, with even journalists reportedly getting stuck in by "throwing debris from the sidelines".

Better late than never . . .

Being kept waiting doesn't engender good temper and things spilled over after Scottish side Falkirk endured a 150-minute wait to kick off a pre-season friendly in 2006. Turkish side Rizespor showed up at 5.37 pm for a match scheduled for 3 pm. Scuffles soon broke out and officials walked off the field after 22 minutes. They were persuaded to return and Rizespor scored. When Falkirk replied however, Rizespor's goalkeeper Atilla Koca took exception to the celebrations of the Scottish fans behind his goal and quickly became embroiled in a fight with them. The match was abandoned – this time for good.

Perugia sign Gaddafi son

Perugia hit the headlines when they signed the son of Libyan leader Muammar Gaddafi. Midfielder Saadi Gaddafi secured a two-year contract to play for Italian Serie A club Perugia in 2003. Perugia denied the move was a publicity stunt, explaining that Gaddafi was a Libyan international and had been transferred like any other player from another club, this time Ittihad in Libya. Saadi, who already had business relationships with three other Italian clubs including part ownership of Juventus, said: "The work in front of me isn't easy but this is an opportunity I couldn't pass up."

Tongue-tied

Honduran defender Brayan Beckeles denied using his tongue when he kissed Vida team-mate Orlin Peralta on the lips during a goal celebration. "Nothing went in or out," Beckeles said.

Rous ousted by intransigence

Intransigence led to the downfall of one of the most powerful men in football history. Englishman Sir Stanley Rous, as the president of FIFA, refused the request of African members to guarantee them a place in the 1966 World Cup staged in England. Rightfully indignant, the African nations boycotted the qualifying tournament, which led to rank outsiders North Korea getting to the finals. But Rous' comeuppance was to follow eight years later. His high-handed approach to the African request had alienated enough federation representatives world-wide for them to vote against him when challenged by Brazilian Joao Havelange.

Gun charge

Xerez president Joaquin Bilbao resigned from the Spanish La Liga club over allegations he conducted a drive-by shooting at a brothel. "I have a completely clear conscience" he said.

Politics beat football

The Soviet Union boycotted a 1973 World Cup qualifying play-off with Chile because it was played in the Santiago Stadium. What the Russian had against the stadium was that it had been used as a brutal torture centre and concentration camp when Salvador Allende's Marxist government was overthrown. Intense diplomatic activity within the higher echelons of football circles failed to break the impasse and the Soviet Union refused to budge. As a result the Chileans were given a walkover to reach the 1974 World Cup finals in Germany.

Bosman's the boss

"Moving on a Bosman" came into the language of soccer in 1995. A revolution in modern football was sparked by a player who never hit the heights of top leagues or the international stage, but became an international rebel with a cause and turned the administration of the game on its head. Belgian Second Division player Jean-Marc Bosman was furious that his club, Liege, demanded a fee beyond the means of Dunkerque in France, who wanted to sign him at the end of his contract. Hearings about his complaint ruled against Bosman before a civil court ruled in his favour that it was illegal to hold a player for a fee beyond his contract. Thousands of players have since moved free "on a Bosman".

Sweet FA for Preston

Coming clean about paying their players during the early English league's amateurism period cost Preston North End dear. One of the league's earliest major disciplinary actions against a football club was in 1894 when Preston admitted paying players. Indignant North End were barred from the prestigious FA Cup for a season and complained that they were not the only northern-based club paying wages illegally. However, the scandal forced the FA's hand and within months professionalism was legalised. Previously, amateur clubs that felt strongly about payments to players unsettling the game had threatened to boycott the 1893–94 FA Cup.

Ref's red card – for himself

Referee Andy Wain is a man who stuck to the letter of the football law, so when he lost his temper while officiating he sent himself off. After awarding a goal to Royal Mail AYL in an English Sunday league match the opposition goalkeeper protested. Wain reacted by throwing down his whistle, pulling his shirt out and eyeballing the player and then, as incredulous spectators and players looked on, he sent himself off. Without the official, who admitted off-field personal problems, the game had to be abandoned. Wain said later: "If a player did that I would send him off – so I had to go."

Stolen kit

Thieves who broke into the Irish Football Association's headquarters in Belfast in 2007 stole hundreds of new Northern Ireland football shirts and shorts, which cost the organisation thousands of pounds in lost sales.

Explosive striker

Manchester City's maverick striker Mario Balotelli took on an extra duty in 2011 when he became an ambassador warning children about the dangers of playing with fireworks. But he had to almost burn down his luxury home in order to get the role. Controversial Balotelli got a rocket from his manager Roberto Mancini after his rented home in Manchester's stockbroker belt was badly damaged in a firework prank. The 21-year-old Italian and his friends escaped unhurt after fleeing a blaze started by fireworks being set off in his bathroom. Balotelli reportedly told club officials that he and four friends had been letting off fireworks through an open window at the house.

Food for thought

Steaua Bucharest's owner Gigi Becali is reported to have commissioned a reproduction of *The Last Supper* with himself as the Christ figure.

Oldest hooligan jailed

A man of 56 became England's oldest football hooligan when he was jailed in 2008. The London man was seen on CCTV kicking a police horse during a riot and was jailed for five years. The riot broke out after Millwall, notorious for its violent fans, lost 1–0 to Birmingham City. The man, convicted of riot, was seen running at police lines and encouraged others to build a barricade of wheelie bins to hinder charging police horses. The two hours of violence left 157 police officers and 26 police horses injured. The former match steward was also banned from all football grounds in England and Wales for eight years.

A roar deal for mascot

As an experienced referee in England's premier leagues Mike Riley had dealt with the toughest of players, but he will always remember the day he red-carded – a lion. During Reading's 1–0 win over Newcastle United in 2007, Riley dismissed the home mascot, the lion-suited Kingsley Royal. His "offence" was that he was wearing Reading's blue and white hooped shirt and was confusing match officials. There was more than a hint of irony when Reading coach Steve Coppell commented on the 7-foot-tall lion's dismissal: "I can see where the referee was getting confused. He does look like so many of my players."

Mascot cops the lot

One of the worst disciplinary records for an English soccer mascot is held by one in a policeman's uniform. Bury FC's Robbie the Bobby kept finding himself in the thick of the action – and often on the wrong side of soccer laws – culminating in being sent off three times in as many months in 2001. Robbie's escapades included a 30-yard dash and belly flop when Bury scored against Bristol City, twice performing his infamous "mooning" celebration and being sent off for a fight with Cardiff's City mascot Barclay the Bluebird. Robbie narrowly avoided a fourth red card for pulling the ears off Peterborough's rabbit mascot.

Mascot is celebrity bad boy

The life of a Welsh club's mascot took on soap-opera proportions that included marriage, violence and even an acting career. Things seemed to go to the head of 9-foot-tall Cyril the Swan after he was voted "Best Mascot" by soccer magazine readers. The official mascot of Swansea City was in trouble with the police – mainly for fighting with other mascots and in one incident he ripped off the head of a rival mascot and drop-kicked it into a stand, for which he was fined. Stardom beckoned when Cyril appeared as the Emperor's pet in a pantomime production of Aladdin and married Cybil the Swan in a special ceremony at Swansea's ground, which led to a range of soft toys.

TV porn break

Italian TV channel La7 caused a furore after coverage of a Kosice–Roma match was interrupted by an hour-long hard-core porn movie. La7 alleged sabotage.

Heel hell for Argyle

English Third Division club Plymouth Argyle felt aggrieved when a referee scored the only goal of a match and cost them points. Referee Ivan Robinson, the official at Argyle's Third Division game at Barrow in 1968, had more influence on the result than he imagined. In the 77th minute, with the score at 0–0, George McLean's mishit shot across the Plymouth goal area was seemingly a routine collection for Plymouth goalkeeper Pat Dunne. As the ball headed his way the referee tried to jump out of the way, but only succeeded in a perfect back-heel into the unguarded Plymouth net.

No Merc-y

An eastern European football club owner denied charges in 2009 of kidnapping three men who stole his Mercedes Benz car.

Gay dilemma

The Turkish FA denied banning a referee for being gay. The official explanation was that as the man was barred from military service because of his sexuality he was also unfit for purpose on the football field.

Rock star kit row

Sunday league football team Queen's Head Rangers from Buckinghamshire got £800 of shirts when indie band Babyshambles front man Pete Doherty sponsored them in 2009. League officials were concerned that a picture of the much-publicised junkie singer and the words "F**k Forever" were on them.

What a raquet

The need to liven up a one-sided friendly in 2003 led to some drastic and unusual action by referee Darren Tulett. In charge of a match in which a French tennis players' XI was trailing a Rest of the World team 4–0 at the Stade de France in Paris, the ref suddenly dribbled the ball 40 yards upfield, before passing to Davis Cup player Michael Llodra. Tulett was on hand to meet the return and to fire it into the top corner from 15 yards, before sounding the final whistle. Tulett's explanation for the bizarre twist? "It was a crap game; I was bored running to and fro and I'll never forget my goal at the Stade de France."

Chain reaction

A player sent off for bad language returned with vengeance in mind – and a chain saw. Anthony Lloyd, 20, who admitted possessing an offensive weapon and fighting in public, was sentenced to a year in prison, suspended for two years, along with being ordered to take part in a drug rehabilitation programme. Furious at being red-carded in a game in England in 2008, Lloyd terrorised fellow player Paul Westwood and administered a cut with the chain saw – albeit a superficial one. Judge Neil Stewart blamed the incident on Lloyd's alleged drug and alcohol abuse.

Stairway to hell

An English footballer hitched a lift back to his hotel with a Spanish motorcyclist after a boozy night on tour. When he couldn't awaken the night porter he grabbed the bike, rode it through a plate glass window and up the stairs. Bad enough that the player needed 50 stitches; he also had the wrong hotel.

Fatal turn

A match-day out ended in death for a football fan who fell from a coach as it sped along a motorway. The 22-year-old is believed to have mistaken an emergency exit door for the toilet. The fan was returning home when he tumbled from the coach travelling at around 65mph and was hit by a car. The coach had been hired by an unofficial supporters' club whose members had been drinking on the three-hour trip to the match and the return.

Gazza to the rescue

Former England midfielder Paul Gasgcoigne tried to get behind police lines in a bid to convince his friend, Raoul Moat, to surrender to officers following an armed stand-off. Police refused to let Gazza pass and the incident ended with Moat taking his own life. Gazza said, 'I'm gutted. He was a good friend of mine."

Talking crap

Werder Bremen keeper Tim Wiese claims adrenalin made him shout "Shit on HSV" into a megaphone following a win over the Hamburg side in 2009.

From defeat to invention

Newcastle United fan Gladstone Adams is reported to have invented car windscreen wipers following his team's 3-1 defeat to Wolves in 1908. Returning home from the match, he found himself in the middle of a snowstorm and fed up with having to pull over to clear his screen with his hand, Adams came up with the idea of mechanized windscreen wipers.

Manager in the doghouse

Jose Mourinho hurriedly left an awards' ceremony to save his dog from arrest. When manager of Chelsea in 2007 he responded to a panic call from his wife because police had raided their home looking for a Yorkshire terrier allegedly in violation of Britain's strict quarantine laws. His wife, Tami, had refused to let police take the animal into quarantine before Mourinho arrived to argue with officers himself. It led to the volatile Portuguese being arrested for obstruction, although no charges were filed. In the meantime, the fugitive bitch, Leya, had disappeared but was later found with relatives in Portugal.

Changing sex – and leagues

A player, who competed as a man for 25 years, won permission to play in an Australian women's soccer league. Originally called Martin he became Martine in a 2005 sex-change operation and in 2007 the 47-year-old human rights' activist received approval from Soccer Tasmania to play in women's soccer. Football Federation Australia said that if the player was legally classified as female, she qualified for women's competitions. She had scored six goals in women's soccer before rival fans discovered her past and asked the state association for clarification.

Fair weather friends

Spoon bender Uri Geller had warned Welsh club Swansea they had evil influences in their Vetch Field ground. The Swans called in a Kenyan circus troupe to perform a dance to drive out malignant forces but it rained and they refused to come out. Swansea were relegated at the end of the 2001 season.

Beckham "booted"

A flying boot might have landed in David Beckham's face, but it also landed a windfall for Manchester United in 2003. The dressing room row with manager Sir Alex Ferguson, after a defeat to Arsenal, left Becks with a cut forehead and an irrevocably broken bond between the midfielder and his mentor. The player was quickly sold off to Real Madrid for £25m. An underlying factor was that Ferguson felt Beckham spent too much time indulging in the celebrity lifestyle with his high-profile wife and former Spice Girl, Victoria. United players have since commented that an angry Ferguson often threw items around the dressing room but this time the boot actually hit the player he was berating.

Joe loses no sleep over "Insomnia"

Name calling with a difference caused player versus manager strife at Newcastle United in 2008 when Charles N'Zogbia objected to being called "Insomnia" by acting coach Joe Kinnear. Even in an industry famous for its nicknames, the slip of the tongue on TV had the French player raging about disrespect and refusing to play again for an unrepentant Kinnear. Newcastle's veteran boss hit back by accusing the 22-year-old of "living in a fantasy land". The winger got his wish and was transferred to Wigan in 2009 and had the last laugh: his new club stayed in the English Premier League while Newcastle were relegated.

Seconds out

Bologna's Giuseppe Lorenzo clocked the then-fastest recorded dismissal in a top-flight European game in 1990 when he was off in ten seconds in a Serie A match with Parma.

Sheer Shearer-power wins

England star Alan Shearer turned the tables on the traditional power struggle that is usually won by managers when relationships break down. Manager Ruud Gullit responded to his failure to deliver his promise of "sexy" football to Newcastle United by dropping fans' favourite Shearer. When Newcastle still lost their next match – ironically to bitter local rivals Sunderland – Shearer spoke out against the dreadlocked Dutch coach. In the power struggle that followed Gullit was sacked but not before he hit back by saying Shearer was overrated.

Stam get stamped on over book

An ill-advised autobiography by Dutch international Jaap Stam wrecked his stability as one of Europe's top centre backs. After three Premier League titles and a European Cup in his three years at Manchester United, his 2001 memoirs revealed dressing room secrets and criticised fellow players. It enraged United manager Sir Alex Ferguson and, although Stam might have been indispensable to the Old Trafford faithful, his literary indiscretions got the giant Dutchman sold within weeks to Italian club Lazio. It was seven years before the protagonists were reconciled when Stam, then retired, returned to his former club as a talent spotter.

Fowler lines up white-line protest

Robbie Fowler's career at English Premiership side Liverpool wasn't to be sniffed at until he tried a very special goal celebration. Angered by persistent, though never substantiated, rumours about cocaine snorting, striker Fowler tried to have his say in an unusual and demonstrative way. After scoring a goal in a 1999 match against Everton, he went on all fours and pretended to snort the white lines around the pitch. It caused an uproar and a rift with manager Gerard Houllier that was never healed. He was increasingly sidelined and eventually transferred to Leeds United.

Mustn't be late

Wrexham were forced by UEFA rules to start off for a 1990 away European Cup Winners' Cup tie with Manchester City 24 hours before. The journey time is 40 minutes.

Team-mates' punch-up

Graeme Souness arrived as manager of Newcastle United determined to instil some spirit. Unfortunately, his midfield duo of Kieron Dyer and Lee Bowyer took "fighting spirit" the wrong way. They punched each other during a match and earned a red card each.

Can't you read?

Everton goalkeeper Richard Wright injured himself warming up before a 2003 game at Chelsea – on a sign telling him not to warm up in the goal area.

Air rage

England players came under fire for their drinking exploits on a 1996 tour to the Far East. They caused £5,000 damage to an aircraft, then some squad members were pictured strapped into a dentist's chair at a Hong Kong club having drinking poured down their throats from a height.

Hard man Billy

A fraud conviction, a self-confessed gambling addiction and rumours of supplementing his income with bare-knuckle boxing were just some of the colourful off-field antics of striker Billy Whitehurst. Some of the biggest names in English football rated Whitehurst the hardest man they had ever played against. Wandering Whitehurst played for nine English league clubs and also in Ulster, Australia and Hong Kong. The former bricklayer cemented his place as a cult figure before a knee injury forced his retirement in 1993, but in 2005 he was convicted of a £12,000 fraud after failing to declare a footballer's pension while claiming unemployment benefit.

Games go flat

Balls burst twice in England's showpiece FA Cup final in successive years. In both the 1946 and 1947 finals at Wembley Stadium, the ball going flat interrupted games before packed crowds. In 1946 Derby County player Jack Stamps might have won the game against London side Charlton Athletic but for the ball bursting as he connected with it, enabling Charlton goalkeeper Sam Bartram to save. It meant the score remained at 1–1 and Derby had to go into extra time to secure a 4–1 win. The next year another burst ball was a luckier omen for Charlton as they scored with the new ball to win 1–0 over Burnley.

Low blow for Sir Alex

Drunken thug Kevin Reynolds was jailed for 15 months in 2007 for punching Sir Alex Ferguson in the groin. Fellow Scot Reynolds pleaded guilty to assaulting the Manchester United manager outside a London railway station and attacking and racially abusing a police officer. The attack left Sir Alex doubled up in pain and the officer, ironically named Peace Toluwa, with a cut upper lip after he was headbutted while trying to restrain Reynolds. In evidence Reynolds was said to have staggered towards the manager before saying, "I'm sorry Fergie. I did not know it was you," but he then chanted: "Fergie, Fergie, shut your mouth" – a football shout common in Scotland.

Who ate all the pies?

Former Arsenal midfielder Paul Merson confessed that the early 1990s team members were not always physically prepared for a hard 90 minutes of Premiership football – sometimes because of pie-eating competitions on the coach to matches.

Jewellery stolen during game

Police were waiting for a defender when he left the field after a game in the Uruguayan league. He was accused of the theft of a gold chain belonging to the opposing team's striker. The striker was famous for wearing gold chains and other jewellery on the pitch and as both players grappled while awaiting a corner kick, the defender ripped off a chain and hid it in his sock. The moment was captured by TV cameras and after the game the defender was arrested. Charges were dropped as he had returned the chain.

Ripping yarn for Norwich fans

It took two fans just 22 minutes of the first match of the 2009–10 English season to become disillusioned. Frustrated as their newly relegated Norwich City fell 4–0 behind to Colchester United, the two fans charged across the pitch, ripped up their £350 season tickets and threw them towards Norwich manager Bryan Gunn. Although stewards and police escorted them out of the stadium there was some sympathy for the fans' frustration, because Coca-Cola League One Norwich went on to suffer their heaviest-ever home defeat, 7–1. Gunn was sacked within days. Ironically, Norwich City were promoted at the end of the season.

Getting shirty

German club Gottingen 05's 2009 shirt deal caused a storm because it advertised – a brothel. After problems getting a conventional backer, club director Burkhard Bartschat said: "We have 700 children at matches – but so what? It's real life. People should grow up."

Magician Mavuba

Zaire dead-ball specialist of the 1970s Mafuila Mavuba would place a coloured hankie over the ball when taking a free kick, then whip it off magician-like before shooting.

Suit-able punishment

Ian Holloway, manager of English Coca-Cola Championship side Blackpool, was forced to wear an oversized £12.99 charity shop suit in 2009 as a forfeit for being late for training.

Lille star is carjack victim

Lille striker Pierre-Alain Frau ended up in a different kind of boot when he fell victim to carjackers. Robbers posing as police locked the French striker in the boot of his Mercedes car and drove off. He was dumped in another part of town but his expensive car was stolen. Frau had been on his way home from a late-night dinner after Lille's 2–1 2009 Ligue 1 defeat by Lorient. As well as his car, his credit card, mobile phone and hundreds of euros were also stolen. It was the second time in ten months that Frau had been targeted by carjackers.

Police quell players' riot

Riot police used pepper sprays and truncheons to break up a fight at a Brazilian championship match in 2008. And it wasn't the fans who were scrapping but the players at Nautico's home game with Botafogo. The match was interrupted for 12 minutes by the fighting, which ended with Botafogo defender Andre Luis being arrested but released after questioning. Trouble erupted when Luis was dismissed and the furious player made gestures to Nautico supporters and kicked a plastic bottle into the stands. He was surrounded by riot police before other Botafogo players intervened and a free for all started. Nautico won 3–0.

Praying for luck

Oxford United organised a prayer of exorcism in the centre circle of their ground in order to stem a run of poor home form after moving to a new stadium.

Night-mayor experience

A school's world record bid came to a disappointing end with a scuffed kick by the local dignitary invited to seal the attempt in 2012. Sure-footed students at St Columba's College in St Albans had clocked up 649 consecutive passes and invited Mayor Aislinn Lee to make the 650th kick – and she fluffed it. Under pressure after being told that even two boys on crutches had completed their passes, her shot travelled barely half the 11m distance required. Fortunately the boys were not relying on Lee to clinch the £50,000 charity drive – they had already passed the previous record of 579 before bringing on the mayor.

Ray's last laugh

The official explanation for Ray Harford's sacking by Luton Town in 1990 was that he was "dour" and lacked "the charisma or ability to relate to fans". He had the last laugh because he had just signed a two-year contract.

Brazil players are kidnap targets

The price of fame for Brazilian footballers has been borne by their relatives who have become the targets of ruthless kidnap gangs. In 2004 the mother of Robinho, Marina de Souza, was kidnapped from her home near Santos and was held for a month before being released. It was claimed that a ransom was paid. In the same year there were happy outcomes for the mothers of Sao Paulo striker Grafite, Porto striker Luis Fabiano and Fidelis Rogerio, who were all were released unharmed.

Quick work

English league hard man Vinnie Jones was booked with his first illegal tackle in an FA Cup game between Chelsea and Sheffield United. Four seconds were on the clock.

Police free kidnapped sister

Police rescued the sister of AC Milan striker Ricardo Oliveira who was held hostage by kidnappers in Brazil for five months. One of the longest kidnappings in the country's history ended when an anonymous tip led police to where Maria de Lourdes Oliveira was being held in an impoverished suburb of Sao Paulo. The 35-year-old was malnourished, dehydrated and ill-treated by her kidnappers, who escaped police. The 2007 kidnapping came a month after striker Oliveira left Spanish club Betis for Milan.

Appetite for success

Food psychology almost worked for Chile in the 1962 World Cup finals. They beat Switzerland, Italy and Russia after consuming pre-match cheese, pasta and vodka respectively. Drinking coffee, however, did not get them past Brazil in the semi-final.

Caught short

Alan Wright, Aston Villa's diminutive full back from 1995 to 2003, once injured his knee and was sidelined because the accelerator on his Ferrari was awkwardly placed for his 5-foot 4-inch size. When he recovered he bought a Rover.

Fatal shot

A player was shot dead by a spectator as he was about to score an equalising goal. The incident happened in the last minute of an Iraqi league match between two local rivals in March 2009.

Crespo's rubbish idea

Argentinian striker Hernan Crespo once revealed a secret of wanting to be a refuse collector. The much-travelled star, who has played for English, Argentinian and Italian clubs, said being a bin man was his dream as a boy growing up in Buenos Aires. It was inspired by watching the city's garbage collectors at work from his bedroom window. "The garbage man would drive past my house with his horse and cart. I loved that. I imagined myself going around the city, driving the cart," he told The Sun newspaper. It is unlikely that the city authorities of Buenos Aires would pay him the £90,000 a week he earned at his peak.

Strike costs striker £10m

It was estimated that a three-month strike by Manchester City's Carlos Tevez may have cost him £10m in lost wages and club fines. The disgruntled Argentinian goalscorer became a striker in the more literal sense when he refused to come on as a substitute in a 2011 Champions League tie. Further clashes with manager Roberto Mancini and his employers caused Tevez to disappear to Argentina for months. He returned to the club in the spring of 2012 and was gradually rehabilitated, winning his place back just as the team lost its lead at the top of the Premiership and were dumped out of the Europa League. Upon his return Tevez struck up a lethal partnership with fellow Argentine Sergio Aguero to help lead Manchester City to their first league title in 44 years.

Costly booze snooze

Newcastle United fan Paul Dalzeil spent £340 on an away trip to watch his beloved side play in the 2002–03 Champions League – and didn't see a kick. As delirious fellow Geordies celebrated Newcastle's 3–1 win over German side Bayer Leverkusen, Paul, 42, snoozed his way through the entire 90 minutes. He admitted he had drunk a little too much to calm his pre-match nerves and proclaimed himself "gutted" at failing to stay awake for a single kick of the game. What he missed was a Newcastle demolition of the Germans in one of the English side's best European performances.

Ref threatens players with axe

A referee flipped more than a coin at a match in London. The official flipped his lid when abusive players got the better of him – and he threatened them with an axe. He abandoned the five-a-side game between Romark FC and Czech Club in Finchley, ran off the pitch and returned moments later stripped to the waist and waving a long axe around his head. An eyewitness said: "All hell broke loose. The ref was like Conan the Barbarian. When a player called him a fairy he went completely berserk." The unnamed ref scattered the players – hurting no one – got in his car and drove off.

Principled football stand

Berlin club FC Union – famous for its anti-Communist stance in the former East Germany – scrapped a €10m sponsorship deal after it emerged that the head of the sponsoring firm was an ex-Stasi officer.

Heads you lose

Clydesdale Bank Scottish Premier League side Falkirk lost their heads – or rather their mascot did in 2009. The head worth £1,000 was stolen from the club's Westfield Stadium.

Vegetable vengeance

Police started a hunt for two fans who bombarded opposition supporters with celery at a Scottish league match. Just before the start of a 2003 Berwick Rangers clash with Stranraer, the two supporters ran out behind the teams and started lobbing sticks of celery at visiting fans in the centre stand at Shielfield Park. The pair were thrown out by stewards, but got away before the police, who believed the incident was retaliation for a corresponding fixture at Stranraer when coins were thrown, could get their hands on them.

Player's legal own goals

A Premiership footballer's bid to protect his private life with a super-injunction backfired massively in 2012. The married international wanted to keep his extra-marital affair secret but his name was revealed by an MP, protected under House of Commons privilege. More embarrassment followed when details of a different affair – a long-term one not covered by the injunction – were published in the media. The player then lost a damages claim against the original woman because she was able to prove that she never planned the "kiss and tell" interview the player feared and which prompted the super-injunction in the first place.

Nuts about Brazil

Two Chinese pensioners went on a rampage in Nanjing after Brazil were defeated by France in a World Cup quarter-final. One ran amok, hitting bystanders with a stick and biting others. The other ran naked carrying a banner reading "Brazil Must Win".

John tramp-les ambitions

Striker John Fashanu used the quick-thinking he was famous for on the pitch to secure the £1.25m home of his dreams. Faced with having to queue for two days with other millionaires to bid for the apartment in London's Knightsbridge he sought help – from a street person. Fash the Bash, as the hard man was known during his English league-playing days with Wimbledon, Millwall and Aston Villa, paid a tramp £300 to hold his place in the queue. The tramp was as good as his word and turned down rival offers of more than £2,000 so England international Fashanu got his flat.

Totting up the money

Although adored as a player in Italy, AS Roma's Francesco Totti is the butt of comedians' jokes alluding to him not being intelligent. He is, however, bright enough in financial terms and has turned the situation to the advantage of several charities. At the suggestion of friends, he helped compile a book of jokes about himself called All the Totti Jokes. It sold 500,000 copies soon after its 2003 launch and continues to sell. Money from the sales went to a project helping the elderly in Rome and to a Unicef project helping homeless children in the Democratic Republic of Congo. An example of a Totti joke? What were the three hardest years for Totti? Class one in elementary school.

Hand of God II?

Having a hand in the winner took on a different meaning for France striker Thierry Henry in a World Cup play-off against the Republic of Ireland in 2009. TV replays showed French captain Henry controlling the ball with his hand, not once but twice, before passing for William Gallas to score a face-saving goal. The Gallas goal meant France scraped into the 2010 World Cup in South Africa on the back of a 2–1 aggregate over two games. Demands by Irish politicians for the match to be replayed fell on deaf FIFA ears but there was also a nationwide call in Ireland for a boycott of French goods.

Crafty move

A goalkeeper who tried to use witchcraft to turn the tide of a match his side was losing sparked a brawl that killed 11 in the Congo. Spectators who threw rocks had tear gas fired on them by police and the 11 died in the rush to the exits.

Working in union

Fans of German third division side Union used their pooled skills to rebuild their stadium – 1,500 supporters put in 95 per cent of the work free and saved their club €2m.

Inclement Weatherly

With overnight snow in 1987 preventing him driving, Gillingham captain Mark Weatherly trudged six miles to the ground – only to find the match called off.

Streaker pays high price for his fun

The cost of dancing naked into the middle of a match was considerable for Mark Hargreaves. The Burnley fan lost his job, his girlfriend, £250 and was banned from grounds for three years. The former professional boxer, who had several drinks on the day of the offence, pleaded guilty to pitch encroachment and was fined £200 with £50 costs for break-dancing on the pitch at Turf Moor during a televised FA Cup fifth-round tie against Blackburn Rovers in 2005. Asked why he did it, he replied: "For a laugh."

Penalty penalised

An plan to re-invent penalty-taking was foiled in Japan's J-League in 2010. Hiroshima defender Tomoaki Makino placed the ball and shaped up for a run up when striker Hisato Sato rushed past him to score. The referee ruled it out for unsportsmanlike behaviour.

What a shame!

The response of players in China's Super League to FIFA's international Fair Play Day was a series of assaults on referees. Seven players were fined, one was banned for eight games and another for four games after throwing a boot at a referee.

Dangerous mom

Police revoked the firearms permit of an American mother who openly carried a gun at her children's soccer practice sessions. The decision was later overturned by a judge and tragically Meleanie Hain was shot by her husband.

Stack attack beats off angry fans

English goalkeeper Graham Stack was used to punching the ball away from his goal, but in the 2002–03 season his fists came in handy to save himself from rioting fans. Although he was Arsenal's reserve goalkeeper, he won cult status while on loan at Belgian club Beveren for thumping a supporter from rivals Royal Antwerp. After being subjected to abuse and missile throwing during the game Stack confronted Antwerp fans who menacingly ran on to the pitch to confront him at the final whistle. Claiming self-defence, he punched one of them in the face. He was quoted as saying: "Someone was running at me and it was obvious he wasn't going to stop. I swung at him out of self-defence."

What a swine!

An Icelandic premier league match was postponed in October 2009 because eight players from FC Grindavik contracted swine flu.

Are you Sitton uncomfortably?

English league player John Sitton didn't enjoy spectacular success as a club manager but earned fame for sacking a player at half-time. He was manager of Leyton Orient when it was the subject of a 1995 TV "fly-on-the wall" documentary. After a poor first-half performance by the London side, he was filmed sacking the player. He also offered to fight defender Terry Howard and another player, and was quoted as shouting, "You can bring someone else to help you, and you can bring your f*****g dinner."

Belgian unrest blames Franky

As a player Franky Vercauteren was revered in Belgium, but his reputation dipped within days of becoming Belgium's international coach. A celebrity website reported him dead, then stories of player unrest seeped out. Belgium's "Red Devils" were earning their devilish reputation as much off the field as on, with reports of players feigning injury to go clubbing, while some refused to travel unless allowed to carry Gucci man bags. As Belgium's 2010 World Cup campaign hit rock bottom a fight broke out between players in a nightclub after the 5–0 defeat in Spain, and players were also seen drinking before the 2–1 defeat in Bosnia-Herzegovina. Even the fans voted with their feet when just one travelled to a match in Armenia. Vercauteren resigned after failure to qualify for the 2010 World Cup.

30-year silverware mystery solved

A soccer mystery that persisted for decades was solved in 2009. England star of the 1970s, Stan Bowles had been touted, even in his autobiography, as the player who had deliberately dented the coveted FA Cup when he took a pot shot at it during the warm-up for a game. It had been on display at 1976 cup winner's Sunderland's game with Bowles' Queen's Park Rangers when the silver cup was knocked over, upsetting the rightly proud home fans. Many years later Gordon Jago, QPRs' manager at the time, said the whole thing was an accident.

We're off

Ethiopia was effectively stripped of its national team when 16 members of the squad sought political asylum in Italy. Fifteen players and their coach disappeared from Rome en route to an Africa Cup of Nations match in Morocco in 1997.

On the run

Hours before the kick-off of a 2004 charity match against Italian side Verona, nine members of the 15-man Afghan national squad disappeared. Gate money from the match – which went ahead by drafting in players from Germany and Britain – had been due to go to a Kabul hospital.

Bunged out of work

Arsenal sacked manager George Graham in a "bung" scandal in 1995. He was accused of creaming off money from transfers in an illegal arrangement with an agent – colloquially known in Britain as a "bung". After a Premier League inquiry found him guilty of taking £425,000 from agent Rune Hauge, Graham, a former Arsenal player, was banned from all football for a year. The money came from the transfers of Scandinavian players John Jensen and Pal Lydersen to Arsenal.

Scoring's a piece of cake

Brazilian star Neymar expected pats on the back from colleagues when he notched the 100th goal of his career on his 20th birthday. His Santos teammates had a double-celebration cake ready for him but forgot to bake it and instead covered him in lashings of flour and chocolate sauce. The only black spot on Neymar's day was that Santos lost 2-1 to Palmeiras in the 2012 Brazilian league match.

Weigh to go

A boxing-style weigh-in decided the fee when Kenneth Kristensen moved between Norwegian league clubs Vindbjart and Floey in 2002. The deal was Kristensen's weight in fresh shrimp.

True or false?

A story came out of war-torn Iraq in 2005 that an Englishman was saved from being shot by insurgents because he had a car sticker with the Portsmouth badge, which has a Muslim-style crescent and star.

Gnash of the day

A dog called Bryn is probably the only animal ever credited with saving a team from relegation. Torquay United were playing on the last day of the season in 1987 and facing the drop out of the English league altogether. With Torquay trailing 2–1 to Crewe Alexandra, in the final few minutes police dog Bryn, who was patrolling the touchline with his handler, bit Torquay's Jim McNichol's thigh. It took four minutes to treat the wound and in the fourth minute of injury time Torquay striker Paul Dobson grabbed a dramatic equaliser, which saved his team. After his death, Bryn was stuffed and put on display in the Torquay boardroom.

Marco turns off

2006 World Cup winner Marco Materazzi did not even watch his beloved Italy defend their title in 2010. The 36-year-old who was out of the national squad spent the time touring the USA in his motorhome.

Egg explosion

Glasgow Rangers defender Kirk Broadfoot had to be treated in hospital for facial injuries caused – by an egg. He was poaching an egg in his microwave in 2009 when it exploded and scalded him.

Barred from the bench

There was an expensive disappointment for a German fan who paid £1,500 to join his idols on their team bench – only to be told there was no room. Manfred Adelmann thought he had secured a place on the Eintracht Frankfurt bench for the match against Union Berlin after outbidding hundreds of other fans in an auction. Then the bureaucrats of the German Football League barred it saying it was against regulations because only 15 people were allowed on a team's bench. Union Berlin saved the day for Manfred by giving him access to their VIP section.

Hair-brained idea

If Tottenham Hotspur striker Gary Lineker had not scored in the first half of a match he would hope to change his luck by changing his shirt. He also reckoned a goal drought could be ended by a haircut.

Historic result for Faroe Islands

Austria will forever be known as the first side to be defeated by the little Faroe Islands. The European Championship group-qualifying match in 1990 was the islanders' first recognised FIFA international and the team of amateurs won 1–0 thanks to timber merchant Torkil Nielsen's goal. The match was played in Landskrona, Sweden, because the islands (population 48,000) did not have the facilities to host it. The Faroes, situated between Iceland and Norway, had joined FIFA only two years before, but had played unofficial games since the 1930s.

Baggio's miss is point of principle

Roberto Baggio refused to take a penalty against a former club he had been devoted to. When Baggio was transferred from Fiorentina to Juventus in Italy's Serie A, adoring Florence fans rioted. The crunch came when potent penalty taker Baggio was expected to take a spot kick against his beloved old club – and he refused. His thinking was that if he missed it would look as though he was favouring his old side. His stand-in missed anyway and Juventus lost 1–0. Juve coach Luigi Maifredi was so furious with Baggio he immediately substituted the player.

Armed and dangerous

Steve Morrow found himself injured during goal celebrations as his team Arsenal won England's League Cup in 1993. Morrow's ecstatic captain Tony Adams had picked up the Northern Ireland international after he scored the winning goal in a 2–1 win against Sheffield Wednesday – then dropped him. Instead of joining the trophy presentation and lap of honour with his team-mates, Morrow found himself being ferried to hospital in an ambulance for treatment to a broken arm. Shame-faced Adams said: "Accidents can happen in moments of ecstasy."

Drug bust

A Nigerian man arrested in India claimed he got involved in drug trafficking because of his love of soccer. He told police that he agreed to carry 500 grams of heroin for the chance of a career in India.

Eric's kung-fu revenge

Eric Cantona's flying kung-fu attack on an abusive fan made headlines around the world in 1995. Manchester United's volatile French star had been sent off for punching Crystal Palace defender Richard Shaw, with whom he had had a running battle all evening. Then Cantona snapped again when he was abused by Matthew Simmons in the packed crowd and he launched a kung-fu kick and followed up with a punch tos the Palace fan's face. Cantona received a total of ten months' bans imposed by his club and the Football Association and ended up in a criminal court, where he was given community service.

The word of Jesus offends

The verbal violence of Atletico Madrid president Jesus Gil landed him with an eight-month ban from all club duties. The Spanish soccer authorities finally lost patience with Gil's outbursts in which he insulted referees and football officials. Gil called one ref a homosexual and then accused referees of ganging up against his club. He said of them: "There's a mafia in refereeing. Competition is disturbed and prostituted. They rob you and you can't do anything about it." Football disciplinary authorities said his words were "the worst example of verbal violence in Spanish sport".

Shining example

Bristol City's follically-challenged goalkeeper of the 1980s, John Shaw, reckoned floodlight glare bounced off his shiny pate and distracted opposing strikers in one-on-one situations.

Cash incentive

A 12-year-old schoolboy offered Ipswich Town his pocket money to try to tempt star player Matt Holland to stay. Martin Lambert offered his £5 weekly allowance to help towards the player's £15,000-a-week wages. It didn't work – Holland moved to Charlton Athletic.

Tyred out

A road crash in China was blamed on the 2002 World Cup finals. The driver of a truck carrying construction materials blamed his crash on the Shanghai–Ningbo highway on driving long hours in order to get home in time for a semi-final.

Bee off

Bees halted a 2009 Mexico–El Salvador World Cup qualifier when a swarm invaded a goalmouth. The match was just three minutes old when the bees arrived and play was held up for six minutes as fire extinguishers were used to clear the insects. Mexico won 4–1.

Own-goal death sentence

Colombian defender Andres Escobar was murdered ten days after his own goal condemned his team to an early World Cup exit in 1994. The goal led to a 2–1 defeat to the hosts USA and Colombia, one of the pre-finals' favourites, going home at the group stage. Gunmen shouted "Goal!" each time they fired 12 shots into Escobar in an ambush in a restaurant car park in the city of Medellin. The player, known by fans as "The Gentleman of Soccer", is believed to have been targeted by accomplices of a gambler who lost heavily on Colombia's early exit.

Make it snappy

The coach of Zimbabwean side Midlands Portland Cement tried to restore harmony by sending his 17-man squad into the crocodile-infested Zambezi River for a ritual cleansing. One player never came out and they lost their next match.

Two-day cup final

A Spanish cup final lasted two days in a bizarre splitting of play. At the 1995 Copa del Rey it was all square at 1–1 between Valencia and Deportivo La Coruna when in the 80th minute torrential rain forced an abandonment of the game. It was decided that the final 11 minutes of the game should be played three days later. The game resumed and the players had barely warmed up before Deportivo scored through Alfredo Santaelena and held on to win 2–1 over the course of the two games for the club's first trophy in their 89 years.

Lethargic move

After only 3,039 fans turned up to watch Wimbledon play an English Premier League home game, the club made plans to move 60 miles north to Milton Keynes and emerged as MK Dons.

Same again, John

Chelsea and England captain John Terry makes sure to use the same urinal in the dressing-room toilets and if the spot is taken he will wait until he can use it, even if others are free.

No-show farce

Scotland players got changed, warmed up and went out on to the pitch – and found the opposition weren't coming. Estonia refused to turn up for a brought-forward kick-off time for a 1996 match in Talinn. With the Estonian squad still at their training camp 60 miles away, Yugoslav referee Miroslav Radoman farcically allowed the Scots to kick off – then blew the final whistle. Scotland had successfully won an earlier start because they complained the stadium floodlights were inadequate. Estonia refused, literally, to play ball and while Scotland should have been awarded the match 3–0 under FIFA rules, it was replayed in Monaco and ended goalless.

Fowler's honesty policy

One of England's most prolific strikers of the 1990s argued against a penalty in his favour. As he went for goal, the Liverpool player tripped as he rounded Arsenal goalkeeper David Seaman. The referee pointed to the penalty spot despite there being no contact by the keeper. Fowler, a player with a bad-boy image, argued that it wasn't a penalty but the referee was adamant. Fowler was Liverpool's principal penalty taker and offered only a soft shot, which Seaman saved. But the fates were determined Liverpool were to win as Jason McAteer scored with the rebound. The 1997 game ended 2–1.

Brolly good goal

As his Aston Villa side played Sheffield United in atrocious conditions in 1901, winger Charlie Athersmith borrowed an umbrella from a spectator and even, brolly in hand, scored a goal.

Grave admission condemns ref

Crooked Spanish referee Emilio Guruceta Muro's sins were revealed – ten years after his death. English club Nottingham Forest suspected bias by the referee when they lost 3–0 to Belgian club Anderlecht in a UEFA Cup semi-final second-leg match in 1984. They felt there was more than bad refereeing, but nothing was proven. Muro died in a car crash in 1987 and a decade later former Anderlecht president Constant Vanden Stock admitted to loaning Muro one million Belgian francs.

Frustrated fan shows the pros how

Indonesian football fan Hendri Mulyadi took matters into his own hands as he watched his national team's inept performance. Cheered on by a 40,000-strong crowd in Jakarta, he vaulted advertising hoardings, got control of the ball and raced down the wing before Oman's keeper blocked his shot. He did not get the chance to try again as police overpowered him. Mulyadi, 25, acted as his team was heading for a 1–2 defeat against Oman, which meant Indonesia failing to reach the finals of the Asian Cup for the first time since 1992. He later apologised.

Tiger Cup stitch-up revealed

Thailand and Indonesia ganged up to try to stop Tiger Cup hot favourites Vietnam from qualifying for the next round by both trying to lose. In the competition for South-East Asian nations Thailand and Indonesia were through to the semi-finals and did not want a strong Vietnam alongside them. In a game of bad defending a deliberate own goal by Indonesia's Mursyid Effendi gave the Thais a 3–2 win. In the inquiry that followed he was banned for life and both countries, which lost their semis, were fined $40,000 each for "violating the spirit of the game".

Losing team get a real barracking

Getting on the wrong side of a military dictator can be a problem as the Ivory Coast national team found in 2000. After a 3–0 defeat to Cameroon saw them crash out in the first round of the Africa Cup of Nations, the Ivorian leader General Robert Guei held the team in a military barracks for several days and berated them for "behaving unworthily" and bringing shame on the country. He told the side that they would be conscripted into military service if they didn't improve and get some pride back. FIFA condemned the threat and the players lasted longer than Guei, who was deposed months later.

Left-wing urinal

The pre-match good luck ritual for German striker Mario Gomez was always to use the urinal situated furthest to the left.

Fishy tale

Fulham player liaison officer Mark Maunders revealed in 2005 that he was once called to the home of a panicky French player to sort out why his fish were swimming in the wrong direction in their bowl.

Bread fears

Wolverhampton Wanderers manager of the 1970s Bill McGarry did not like players eating prawns because he thought they weakened the stomach. Similarly, he allowed only one bread roll per man because he thought they slowed his players down.

Code of honour

The spirit of fair play did nothing for the win ratio of staunchly amateur English football club Corinthians. This gentlemen's team founded in 1882 played on the principles of amateurism and fair play. So much so that they refused to join the professional game or even to enter the much-coveted FA Cup competition. They dug their studs in even further when penalty kicks were introduced in 1891. If awarded a penalty they would not take advantage of the bonus, neither would the team defend a penalty awarded against them.

Left in the lurch

Goalkeeper Herby Arthur found himself all alone facing 11 opposition players when his team-mates stormed off in a controversial match in 1891. The bad-tempered English league match between Lancashire neighbours Burnley and Blackburn Rovers saw Rovers players fail to return to the pitch after half-time. When they did deign to reappear 3–0 down, two of their players were sent off reducing them to nine men. The rest of the outfield players walked off in protest, leaving Arthur between the sticks. The referee abandoned the one-sided match and saved Arthur from the avalanche of goals that seemed inevitable. The reasons for the Rovers walkout? They didn't like the cold weather.

Old slapper

Superstitious Dutch legend Johan Cruyff used to slap goalkeeper Gert Bals on the stomach as a good luck omen for an Ajax win. He would also spit his chewing gum into the opposition's half. When he forgot his gum in 1969, Ajax lost the European Cup final to Milan 4–1.

Winning signs

The French team's rituals before winning the 1998 World Cup included having the same seats on the team bus and listening to Gloria Gaynor's "I Will Survive" in the changing room. Defender Laurent Blanc kissed goalkeeper Fabien Barthez's bald head before kick-off.

Smell of success

Former England defender Gary Neville did not change his boots and also wore the same aftershave if he was on a winning run.

Ladies' soccer sensations

The Dick Kerr Ladies travelling soccer show was a sensation of the 1920s. Formed from the female employees of a railway equipment company during World War 1, the playing phenomenon attracted as big crowds as male soccer for a short period after the war. A charity match organised at Preston astonished everyone by drawing a crowd of 10,000. Then playing under floodlights with a white ball the women attracted 35,000 spectators at Newcastle's St James' Park and big crowds at the homes of Manchester United and Liverpool. The crowning glory for the ladies was a 53,000 crowd in 1920 at Everton's Goodison Park ground at which 10,000 more were turned away. Their success didn't stop the game's authorities slapping a ban in 1921 on women playing on league grounds.

Taking the piss?

Sergio Goycochea, the former Argentina goalkeeper, urinated on the pitch before facing penalties. It worked well until the 1990 World Cup final.

Ball controversy at first World Cup

Confrontation started before a ball was kicked in the first World Cup final because it was the ball that was the issue. Both Argentina and home side Uruguay wanted a ball made in their respective countries to be used for the prestige occasion. Official rules didn't cover the situation, so the referee tossed a coin and Argentina won. However, there were unconfirmed reports that the Uruguayan ball was used in the second half, which might have inspired Uruguay to come from 1–2 behind at half-time to win 4–2.

Short ritual

Bobby Moore, England's 1966 World Cup-winning captain, insisted on being the last team member to put on his shorts. However, as a joke team-mate Martin Peters would wait until Moore pulled his shorts on, then take off his own. Moore would respond by taking off his shorts and waiting until Peters had put his back on.

German ace saved from Russians

German international inside forward Fritz Walter was saved from certain death in a Russian gulag because a sharp-eyed prison guard had once seen him play. Walter was called up into the German Army during World War 2 and after the defeat of the Nazis found himself a prisoner of war in Hungary. In 1945 when the victorious Soviets started transporting German prisoners of war back to prison camps, where life expectancy was less than five years, the Hungarian guard pointed out that Walter was Austrian. This information meant Walter avoided the gulags and he went on to reach the pinnacle of any football career as captain of West Germany's World Cup-winning side of 1954.

England's 1966 cup hero was a dog

A mongrel dog became the hero of the football world after the Jules Rimet Trophy was stolen prior to the 1966 World Cup finals in England. Pickles, four, sniffed out the gold trophy in bushes near his owner's London home. The 12-inch-high cup had been on pre-World Cup display when it was stolen by Edward Bletchley, who was later jailed. The theft was part of an attempt to demand a £15,000 ransom, but Pickles foiled the plot by finding the statuette wrapped in newspaper. It had been missing for a week and its theft had been a source of acute embarrassment for the English FA in whose care it had been entrusted. The cup was destined to stay in the country as England won it several months later.

Waste not, want not

Former England striker Gary Lineker never took a shot at goal in match warm-ups because he didn't want to waste a goal.

Keeper's on target with seagull

One of the more bizarre mementoes in any football club's trophy cabinet is in the Netherlands – a stuffed seagull. Thousands of fans at the Feyenoord Stadium in Rotterdam witnessed the bird's untimely death in 1970 when a goalkeeper's kick blasted the bird out of the sky. Home keeper Eddy Treytel was the man who entered football folklore with a high kick upfield in a match against Sparta Rotterdam that shot down the bird. After the feathers flew the bird's body was retrieved, whisked off to a taxidermist and it has stood alongside Feyenoord's many domestic and European trophies ever since.

Lucky shirt?

Pelé was so worried by a dip in form that he asked a friend to track down a fan to whom he had given a "lucky" shirt. A shirt was returned, along with the striker's form, but it was later revealed that the search had been futile and Pele had been given another shirt he had previously worn.

Cold comfort

England star David Beckham admitted to an obsessive compulsive disorder in which items have to be arranged just so, even in the fridge. If he has three cans of the same soft drink, he will throw one away to make an even number.

Cruyff's gripes over stripes

There was something different about Johan Cruyff from his Dutch team-mates in the 1974 World Cup. His orange kit sported only two black stripes along the arms and shoulders while the rest of the team had three. The difference was a result of principled Cruyff's dispute over sponsorship. The Netherlands team was sponsored by Adidas but Cruyff, already a superstar and described as "God's gift to football", had his own deal with rival Puma, which he contended he couldn't break. He played in the two-stripe kit while the rest of the team played in Adidas' three stripes.

Socking it to them

Something about Wigan Athletic's Pascal Chimbonda's transfer request smelled. He had kept the written request in his sock throughout a 90-minute match in which Wigan were defeated 4–2 by Arsenal – then whipped the sweaty item out and handed it to manager Paul Jewell.

Dutch minds elsewhere for final

Desperately trying to save marriages and relationships may have been more on the minds of the Dutch team as they faced the 1974 World Cup final against West Germany. Hit by lurid pre-match headlines in German newspapers about naked hotel romps with women and champagne, the Dutch may have been justified in a below-par performance against their European arch-rivals, which they lost 2–1. Although the sex allegations were never substantiated, the Dutch players, including Johan Cruyff, had to face a barrage of phone calls from wives and girlfriends late into the night before the final.

Beach ball wrecks title chances

A beach ball took the bounce out of Liverpool's 2010 Premier League title chances. A fan had thrown the Liverpool-branded ball on to the pitch in a game against Sunderland and it proved crucial because Darren Bent's shot ricocheted off it and into the net for the winning Sunderland goal. Bizarrely, Liverpool's defence including keeper Pepe Reina seemed to follow the beach ball and not the match ball. In the week following there was a rush for the £10 Beach Set and it was feared these were going to Manchester United fans who were planning a mass "tribute" to Bent's goal when the teams next met.

Lost his bottle

Sevilla coach Juande Ramos was knocked unconscious by a frozen hot-water bottle thrown from the crowd at a Real Betis match in 2007.

What a bleeding cheek!

The crowd at Brazil's Maracana Stadium might have initially been fooled but eagle-eyed TV cameramen were not. In 1989, with Brazil leading in a World Cup qualifier, Chilean goalkeeper Roberto Rojas fell dramatically to the ground apparently bleeding from a wound caused by a thrown firecracker. The Chilean team, needing a win against the odds to qualify for the 1990 World Cup finals, stormed off the pitch. But TV replays revealed no flares had landed near Rojas, who had in fact slashed his own scalp with a concealed razor blade. FIFA barred Chile from the 1990 and 1994 tournaments and Rojas and some Chilean officials who helped hatch the plot for life. The Rojas ban was lifted in 2001.

Ref murdered

The incorruptibility of a Colombian league official is believed to have led to his death. Alvaro Ortega was shot dead after running the line in a tense match between Independiente Medellin and America de Cali in 1989. Drug cartels and organised crime were immediately blamed for the murder and the theory was that Ortega had refused a bribe to influence the result between two of the country's major teams. The Colombian league was suspended and despite extensive police investigations no one was brought to justice.

Lucky black cat

A black cat brought luck to Preston North End when it ran on to their pitch in April 2009. Preston ended up 3–0 winners over Brighton in a Coca-Cola Championship game.

Boot revolution started by kids

Out of the mouths of babes. Some childish wisdom – and the destruction of a table tennis bat – led to the creation of the world's bestselling football boot in the early 1990s. While coaching boys in his native Australia, former Liverpool star Craig Johnston was trying to explain how the foot should grip the ball like a table tennis bat in order to swerve it. But one of the kids questioned the logic as boots are made of leather and the instep has no grip when wet. Johnston went home, stripped the rubber off a table tennis bat and super-glued it on to a pair of his old boots. He took the idea to Adidas, who developed the bestselling Predator boot with rubber ridges on the toe.

Chopper commuter

Darren Purse's transfer from West Bromwich Albion to Cardiff City meant family logistical problems so he decided to commute to Wales. He got his helicopter pilot's licence and rented a chopper.

Sting in the tale

A bizarre chain of events led to injuries to spectators at a 2005 match in Zambia. In a scene that could have come straight out of a slapstick movie, celebrating fans climbed a lighting pylon as Zambia scored a second goal in a World Cup qualifier against Congo. The pylon collapsed and, to compound matters, this released a swarm of bees nesting on it. The angry swarm started stinging randomly so spectators tried to escape, fleeing the stands, jumping the perimeter fence and running onto the pitch, disrupting the match which Zambia eventually won 2-0. Fortunately spectators sustained only stings and slight injuries.

Tight fit

Bosnian national team manager Miroslav Ciro Blazevic wore lucky shoes at matches – unfortunately they were two sizes too small.

Rivaldo play-acting upsets Turkey

One of the most incredible pieces of play-acting in order to get a player sent off came in the 2002 World Cup finals. Turkey, already a man down after the sending off of Alpay in the Group C match with Brazil, were reduced to nine men in bizarre circumstances. Brazil striker Rivaldo, who had put the favourites in front, had a ball kicked against his legs by Hakan Unsal, but he amazingly fell, seemingly pole-axed, clutching his face. Rivaldo's bizarre play-acting got Unsal dismissed despite media proof that he was innocent.

Fair-minded Morten pays penalty

Morten Wieghorst blasted a penalty wide in an international between his Denmark national side and Iran – and he missed deliberately. The sparkling example of sporting behaviour came in 2003 when Iranian Jalal Kameli Mofrad mistook a whistle in the crowd for the referee's half-time blast and picked up the ball in his own penalty area. After consulting his coach Morten Olsen, Denmark skipper Wieghorst, believing it morally wrong to capitalise on the mistake, hit the penalty wide. It even meant the Danes would eventually lose to Javad Nekounam's only goal of the game.

Player gets three yellow cards

English referee Graham Poll announced his retirement from internationals after yellow-carding a player three times in a match. The ref, who had sent off players from both sides in a fiery match between Australia and Croatia, carded Josip Simunic twice but did not produce the mandatory red for a sending off. The crowd in Germany for the 2006 World Cup finals group match were incredulous. Poll did not realise his mistake until after the final whistle when he yellow-carded Simunic for a third time and finally produced the overdue red.

Whisky riots destroy Celtic hopes

Glasgow Celtic lost the chance of winning three successive league and cup doubles in 1909 because fans at the Scottish Cup final against Rangers rioted. Rampaging fans, expecting extra time after a drawn match, used whisky to start fires, then slashed the hoses of firefighters who arrived to tackle the blazes. One hundred people were hurt in the mayhem on the neutral ground of Hampden Park and the Scottish FA suspended the cup competition.

Shame of Zidane's finale

The last touch of the illustrious career of Zinedine Zidane was his head knocking the steam out of a giant Italian defender. France's greatest player ended his career on a low note, sent off in front of many millions of global TV viewers in the 2006 World Cup final against Italy. The victim of his powerful headbutt was Italian centre back Marco Materazzi, who was laid out by the force. Zidane claimed Materazzi had insulted his mother. Amazingly the referee missed the off-the-ball incident, which was brought to his attention by the fourth official.

Fangs a lot

A Chelsea fan became a TV star when he was filmed cleaning his teeth on the terraces at a match between his team and Manchester United in 2009. He rang a radio phone-in show to explain he had not had time to brush them before the match.

Amateurs top the world

Twenty years before the Jules Rimet World Cup, a bunch of English amateurs won the original World Championship. Millionaire British tea merchant, Sir Thomas Lipton, put up a World Cup trophy in 1910 to be played in Italy where he had been knighted. The English FA refused to send a team and West Auckland from England's north-east were invited to represent their country. The Northern Amateur League strugglers sold furniture and personal belongings to finance the trip, but beat teams from Switzerland, Germany and the mighty Juventus of Italy to take the trophy. They returned the following year to defend it successfully.

Radio commentary by numbers

The first time league football was brought live to British living rooms was in 1927 when the BBC staged its first radio experiment. Much as today, an announcer gave a running commentary of the action in the Arsenal–Sheffield United First Division game, but he was regularly interrupted by a colleague calling out numbers. Through these numbers listeners could refer to a paper grid they had to identify which part of the pitch play was taking place in.

Nuts to this

A squirrel was an unexpected addition to the crowd in Stevenage's FA Cup fourth-round tie with Bath City in 1999.

Super substitute Stabile shines

Exams gave Argentina's Guillermo Stabile a chance to shine in the 1930 World Cup finals and he grasped the opportunity with both feet. He had replaced captain and centre forward Manuel Ferreira, who had dropped out of the game against Mexico so that he could sit his university exams. Stabile played so well he stayed in the team, forcing Ferreira to move to inside left in the line-up, and finished as the top scorer for the tournament with eight goals. He even scored in the final but could not prevent Uruguay taking the inaugural World Cup 4–2.

Not quack enough

German goalkeeper Sepp Maier's attempt to catch a duck on the pitch during the 1976 Bundesliga match ended in failure. He approached stealthily, leapt arms outstretched – and missed.

Jonathan puts his heart into it

A player scored the winning goal in a game just 24 hours after he had to have his heart started. Jonathan D'Laryea had suffered an unusually high heart rate which medication failed to control so surgeons stopped his heart and restarted it in a successful operation. They cleared D'Laryea to play the next day. The Gainsborough Trinity midfielder celebrated his remarkable recovery with the goal that beat Nuneaton 3-2 in the Blue Square North League and was also voted Man of the Match.

Football the peacemaker

One of the most poignant football matches came on Christmas Day 1915 when, very briefly, peace broke out amid the horrors of World War 1 for a kickabout. German and Allied soldiers climbed from their icy trenches during a ceasefire and exchanged greetings. A football was spontaneously produced and a brief free-for-all game with an estimated 50 or more on each side ensued. It lasted 30 minutes and no score was kept. The mood was broken by a British major who ordered his men back to their trenches and a British artillery bombardment started the killing again.

Taxi attack

London cabbie Joe Hylton was so angry at his team's FA Cup defeat to non-league opposition he marched into the manager's office demanding an explanation. Despite the foul-mouthed exchange, Queen's Park Rangers boss Ian Holloway owned up to his side's shortcomings.

Pheasant hunt

Barcelona fans got a brutal close-up of off-pitch violence in 2002. Unable to trap a pheasant let loose on to the pitch prior to a Champions League quarter-final with Panathinaikos, a steward brutally kicked it against an advertising hoarding and dragged the limp carcass away.

"Trick" telegram thwarts Spain

One of the most bizarre qualifications for a World Cup finals tournament goes to Turkey in 1954. Drawn in a two-team group with Spain, the teams needed a play-off, but after the arrival of a mysterious telegram, Spain's star player Kubala was left out and this gave Turkey the chance of a draw. With everything all square the right of qualification went to lots drawn by a blind Italian boy, which saw Turkey through to the Switzerland finals. The contents of the telegram were never revealed.

Berne-ing tempers in World Cup battle

One of the most disgraceful games in World Cup history involved the cream of footballing talent in the 1954 finals. The quarter-final between the silky skills of Brazil and Hungary became known as "The Battle of Berne" after the Swiss city that staged it. Brazil, 2–0 behind, resorted to violence rather than skill to get back into the game. Hungary retaliated and the game degenerated into a war on the pitch. Incredibly only two Brazilians and one Hungarian were dismissed, but with injuries as well the two sides only had nine effective players each. With Hungary winning 4–2, the final whistle saw a crowd invasion and the fighting carried on between the two teams in dressing rooms and the tunnel.

Tree-mendous devotion

A disgruntled fan of Brazilian side Corinthians took to living in a tree in protest at poor performances. He tied himself into the tree outside the ground, insisting he was staying until results improved.

Match fixers jailed

Ten professional footballers were jailed by an English court in 1965 for their various parts in a match-fixing ring. Sentences ranged from four years for the ringleader to terms between four and 15 months. Among them were England internationals Peter Swan of Sheffield Wednesday and wing half Tony Kaye of Everton. They were found guilty of arranging the outcomes of top matches and were later banned from football for life following a Football Association inquiry. The case came to light after Scottish player Jimmy Gauld admitted in a newspaper article to being at the centre of the conspiracy.

Not fair

The Inter-City Fairs Cup was dubbed the "Not Fairs Cup" after a night of violence in 1966. Leeds United and Valencia were ordered off the pitch for a ten-minute cooling-off period when the match deteriorated into violent play. Police had to intervene when Leeds centre half Jack Charlton was seen chasing an opponent around the pitch. Leeds had had a player severely injured in a previous round against Torino and, in another tie, Chelsea had brawled with Roma players and had their team bus stoned in Italy.

Swarming to see match

A swarm of bees swelled the attendance figures of a match in Brazil in 2011. The discovery of the bees clustering on a crossbar held up play for 20 minutes at the Goiania state championship match between Vila Nova and Goiás. Firemen used a fire extinguisher and a flaming torch to send them away.

Montevideo nasty

Two sides went to war almost literally in the play-off for the World Club Championship in 1968, which ended with six players sent off. European champions Celtic and South American champs Racing Club of Argentina were all square after two matches and the play-off in Montevideo took place in a poisonous atmosphere. Atrocious tackling and violence went on all over the field and police were called to the pitch to stop the sporadic fighting. Racing had two players dismissed but won 1–0, and Celtic had four sent off. Celtic fined their players £250 for their parts in the disgrace; Racing players each got a car.

Moore innocent of theft allegations

England's 1970 World Cup preparations were disrupted by the arrest of their captain Bobby Moore on jewel-theft charges in Colombia. Moore was kept under house arrest after being accused by a Bogota shop girl of stealing an emerald bracelet. She later retracted her statement claiming she was confused, but there were allegations in the Colombian media that Moore, who had denied even seeing the bracelet, was a victim of a plot to frame foreign personalities for the purpose of extortion.

George Best – the cheeky chancer

Northern Ireland's George Best showed his immaculate sense of timing with a cheeky "goal" against England in 1972 that was, incredibly, disallowed. As England goalkeeper Gordon Banks went to kick from his hand, Best nipped in as the ball was between Bank's hand and foot and lobbed it over the keeper's head into the net. The referee disallowed the goal in the England–Northern Ireland international but never explained why. Ironically, England won 1–0 despite being largely outplayed.

Robin's a joker

Zany comedian and actor Robin Williams called FIFA secretary-general Sepp Blatter "Sepp Bladder" when he hosted the draw in Las Vegas for the 1994 World Cup finals.

Gazza's gas

England player Paul Gascoigne appalled Italian fans by burping loudly into a TV reporter's microphone during a 1993 interview about being dropped from the Lazio side.

Scots take the spoils of victory

Mindless Scottish fans celebrated a rare win over England at Wembley Stadium by smashing both sets of goalposts and digging up the famous turf as souvenirs in 1977. Drink and having to watch an ill-tempered match of low technical and tactical quality, led to the Scots being frustrated and wound up by the time the final whistle went on a 2–1 Scottish win. The Scottish horde burst through the pitch-side barriers and invaded the field. Goalposts and nets were soon down and smashed, and many dug chunks out of the grass and pocketed them to take home. Police and security staff took an hour to clear the ground.

Zambia mourns

The entire Zambian national team was wiped out in a plane crash in 1993. The plane taking the squad to a World Cup qualifier in Senegal crashed into the sea killing 30 people.

Jack's tears of frustration

Being bombarded with missiles by his own supporters brought tears of frustration to the eyes of Sheffield Wednesday manager Jack Charlton. He was failing to quell a 1980 riot, which threatened to mar his club's reputation. In a 30-minute stoppage of the game at Oldham Athletic, Charlton pleaded for restraint and was hit with a missile for his trouble. Twenty people, including police, were injured as fans threw concrete and coins and scaled a 2-metre security fence to continue the fight on the pitch. The mayhem had been sparked by the sending off of Wednesday striker Terry Curran.

Stein dies in front of fans

Scotland manager Jock Stein died after watching his side virtually qualify for the 1986 World Cup finals in Mexico. The Scotland supremo collapsed and died from a heart attack in September 1985 in front of thousands of jubilant fans after seeing his team beat Wales in Cardiff. The best-loved man in Scottish football had survived a similar heart attack eight years before. At club level Stein, who was 62 when he died, had made British football history by inspiring Celtic to a 1967 European Cup victory.

Maradona claims Hand of God

Diego Maradona became the highest-profile cheat in football when he punched the ball into the net to "score" against England in front of a global TV audience of billions. Unrepentant, he credited the handball that beat England goalkeeper Peter Shilton to the "Hand of God" as he continued his outrageous gamesmanship long after the final whistle had condemned England to a 2–1 defeat and an early flight home from the 1986 Mexico World Cup finals.

Ireland's dead granny resurrected

Irish international Stephen Ireland "killed" his own grandmother in order to avoid playing for his country so he could visit a girlfriend instead. When the so-called "death" was revealed, Ireland of Manchester City had to resurrect maternal grandmother, Patricia Tallon, fast and apologize. Ireland admitted he had made up a reason to be excused from the Republic of Ireland's 1–0 defeat in the Czech Republic in 2007, in order to visit his "lonely" girlfriend in Cork. He even asked club manager Sven-Goran Eriksson to leave him out of a club fixture because he was still grieving and had to help with funeral arrangements. Eriksson described Ireland as "stupid".

Player violence crackdown

Police across Britain launched a crackdown on violence in football – and a swathe of top professionals ended up in court for their on-field conduct. Rangers and England stars Chris Woods and Terry Butcher and Celtic's Scottish international Frank McAvennie were heavily fined in 1988 for their part in a goalmouth fracas. Police maintained that players' conduct on the field had a direct correlation with fans' behaviour on the terraces. The Glasgow group were found guilty of disorderly conduct and breach of the peace. Twenty-four hours earlier Chris Kamara of Swindon Town was fined £1,200 and ordered to pay compensation for grievous bodily harm to an opposition striker.

War of words

Davor Suker fell out with Real Madrid boss John Toshack in 1999 over transfer dealings at the Bernabeu. The club suspended the Croatian striker without pay, then sold him to Arsenal.

Swindon ups – and downs

Swindon Town's promotion to English football's First Division in 1989 lasted just ten days without a ball being kicked. After winning a play-off final in May to gain promotion to England's elite, the club was relegated two divisions by an FA commission for financial irregularities. After admitting 35 charges of illegal payments to players stretching back four years, Swindon were denied playing Liverpool or Manchester United and forced to meet some of the poorer sides in English football. However, on appeal Swindon's relegation punishment was commuted to the Second Division instead of the Third Division.

Hare we go!

Bulgarian international Hristo Stoichkov chased a hare around Barcelona's pitch during a 1990 match. He was furious that the animal had caused him to stumble and miss a goal opportunity. Stoichkov, though lightning fast, didn't catch it.

Vinnie's video nasty costs him

Welsh hard man Vinnie Jones was handed a massive £20,000 fine by the FA in 1992 for his part in a bestselling video "Soccer's Hard Men". In an interview Jones gave insights into the dirtier and more violent tactics of football. He graphically described how to hurt and intimidate opponents and was fined and given a six-month playing ban suspended for three years. Jones was unlikely to be out of pocket through the fine as the publicity surrounding the disciplinary action boosted sales of the video, which featured Jones' most famous assault of reaching behind him to squeeze Paul Gascoigne's testicles.

Higuita's scorpion kick

Goalkeeper Rene Higuita enlivened a dull 1995 friendly between England and Colombia with his spectacular "scorpion kick" save. With precision judgment he used no hands to save a looping shot by throwing himself forward under the trajectory of the ball and with expert timing kicking up his heels to clear it. The kick was all the rage in the British media next day, and is still a YouTube favourite. The spectacular save ensured the scoreline stayed at 0–0.

Wrong question

When questioned at a 2002 press conference about Sunderland's loss of form manager Howard Wilkinson rounded on a questioner by asking: "What do you know; how many England caps have you won?" "Actually," replied former England captain turned journalist Jimmy Armfield, "43."

Forgot to duck

A duck that interrupted a Finnish first division match between TPS and KuPS in 1993 needed to move "quacker" because it was knocked unconscious by Seth Ablade's corner. Medics revived it and it was able to fly away.

Weight and see

Hard man Neil Ruddock's capacity for eating pies preceded him when he signed for London club Crystal Palace. A clause in his contract said he would be fined if his weight crept over a stipulated limit.

Loan row resignation

The politics at the top of football associations were revealed in a row over allegations of a multi-million pound loan between two FAs. It resulted in the resignation of one of the association's chief executives. Although no impropriety was alleged the row centred on one association promising to loan the association of a neighbouring country £3.2m in return for its supporting a specific candidate's election as a FIFA vice-president. The subsequent row centred on the eight-year loan being promised without the knowledge of other officials of the FA doing the loaning.

Every witch way

The Ivory Coast FA upset witch doctors who claimed they had not been paid for helping the country to a 1992 Africa Cup of Nations win. Strangely, when an alarming slide in form followed, cash and whisky hurriedly changed hands and the country qualified for the 2006 World Cup finals.

Tony revealed as a "fake" Irishman

Tony Cascarino revealed in 2000 that he had been ineligible to play for the Republic of Ireland – after 88 caps and 19 goals for the country. He explained that the news was as much a shock for him as it was for everyone else as the cause was a mix-up over his mother's nationality. The London-born "Irishman" with the Italian name thought he was eligible for Ireland through his grandparents but then found his mother had been adopted by an Irish family and had never secured Irish citizenship for herself. By the time Cascarino had been required by new FIFA rules in 1996 to prove his Irish credentials he had already won 64 caps.

Seventh heaven

Arsenal centre forward Ted Drake scored seven goals in a 7–1 win over Aston Villa in 1935. He also hit the bar and had a goal that crossed the line ruled out – all with an injured and heavily bandaged knee.

Ye olde hooligan

One of the oldest recorded references to a football mis-demeanour is in Henry VIII's time when a drunk was arrested for playing football in a churchyard on a Sunday and for saying he wished the ball was the king's severed head. His fate was not documented.

Costly "Cashley"

A £5m move just a few miles across London for Ashley Cole cost those involved an extra half-million because of the irregularities involved. In 2004 west London club Chelsea were fined a then-record £300,000 after being found guilty of an illegal approach for the left back who was at north London's Arsenal. His employers had no idea Cole, dubbed "Cashley Cole" by Arsenal supporters, had been seeing Chelsea manager Jose Mourinho and chief executive Peter Kenyon without prior permission. The fall-out of the affair was immense, with Cole and Mourinho being fined £75,000 each and Cole's agent Jonathan Barnett fined £100,000 and having his licence suspended for 18 months.

Dozy driver

Derby County's Bob Malcolm stopped his car in the middle lane of England's M1 motorway in 2008 – and went to sleep. He had been drinking, but the actual amount over the legal limit was inconclusive. He was banned from driving for 20 months and fined £750.

Worse for Merson

Any team would think signing up an international player with 21 England caps and seven winner's medals to his credit, including two English Premier League championships, would enhance its squad. But midfielder Paul Merson's March 2012 debut for Sunday league team Whitton Athletic ended in a 6-2 defeat. Merson, who played hundreds of games for Arsenal, Aston Villa, Portsmouth and Middlesbrough, was 43 and admitted to being out of shape since his professional retirement in 2006.

Case of the Spurs "poison" mystery

It would be a job for even Miss Marple or Hercule Poirot to unravel the dark mutterings surrounding a vital Premiership match in 2006. Tottenham Hotspur needed a draw at east London rivals West Ham to secure fourth place – and European football – the following season. In the wings waited bitter north London rivals Arsenal, who stood to take fourth if they won and Spurs lost. The Tottenham team arrived with ten players vomiting, but failed to have the match postponed. Spurs lost 2–1; Arsenal beat Wigan. Lasagne eaten by the team at a hotel the night before was cleared of blame and the cause of the history-changing vomiting virus remained a mystery.

Too-candid Sven trapped by media

Sven-Goran Eriksson's reign as England manager was ended in 2006 – by his mouth. In an interview to an undercover journalist known as the "Fake Sheikh", Eriksson made some injudicious remarks and was released from his England contract two years early. Eriksson spoke frankly about quitting the England role to take over at Aston Villa and suggested that there was corruption within football. There were also personal comments about Manchester United manager Sir Alex Ferguson and England players Wayne Rooney, David Beckham, Rio Ferdinand and Michael Owen.

Bad-boy Barton's lengthening record

The on- and off-field antics of Manchester City and Newcastle midfielder Joey Barton have been surrounded by violence. In 2008 a six-month jail sentence for common assault and affray outside a Liverpool restaurant was followed by a four-month suspended sentence after Barton admitted assault on former team-mate Ousmane Dabo during a training dispute at City. Three days after his release, Barton was charged with violent conduct by the FA for the assault on Dabo. On the field Barton also had an unenviable record of bookings and red cards.

First riot?

A charge by mounted cavalry was needed to break up fighting that had erupted in an 1856 match between Derbyshire parishes All Saints and St Peter's.

For whom the goal tolls

Conspiracy watchers took a keen interest in the occasional goal-scoring heroics of Arsenal midfielder Aaron Ramsey. It seemed that every time the Wales international scored, someone famous died within days. The jinx theory gained even greater currency when singer Whitney Houston died in March 2012 after Ramsey scored against Sunderland. Previously, a May 2011 goal against Manchester United was followed by the death of al-Qaeda terror leader Osama Bin Laden and in October 2011 shortly after Ramsey found the net against Tottenham Hotspur, Apple boss Steve Jobs passed away. In the same month Ramsey struck a Champions League goal against Marseilles – the next day Libyan leader Colonel Gaddafi was shot.

On the trail of St Becks

The Japanese Tourist Board launched plans to market special David Beckham pilgrimage tours because the former English skipper is so popular in the Land of the Rising Sun. The idea was for camera-toting football tourists to visit Salford and Alderley Edge, places that figured in Becks' formative years with Manchester United. It also puts Preston North End on the tourist map as their ground Deepdale was the scene of a Beckham loan spell.

Ruud departure

Ruud Gullit quit the Dutch squad on the eve of their departure for the 1994 World Cup in the USA. An uneasy truce, following a row with coach Dick Advocaat a year before, broke down.

World Cup sparks China crisis

Chinese doctors reported a 20 per cent rise in facial paralysis in Beijing during the 2006 World Cup finals. Although China were not participating, medics believed fans were stressed and exhausted from watching games that were beamed to Chinese TVs from Germany in the early hours of the morning. The condition, known as Bell's Palsy or prosopoplegia, was caused by nerve trauma and was temporary. Most victims recovered in a few weeks or months.

Tail of woe for Chic

Being "tackled" by a dog ended the professional career of goalkeeper Chic Brodie in 1970. The black and white terrier had invaded the field several times but the referee refused to halt proceedings. As the goalie fielded a back pass the mutt decided to chase the ball. Not expecting to see a dog on the pitch running towards him, Brodie kept his eye on the ball and as he bent down to scoop it up the energetic pooch leapt towards the goalkeeper sending him crashing. The ball spun out for a corner, leaving Brodie writhing in agony on the floor with a shattered kneecap and facing the end of his career at 33.

Weah the champion

1995 World, European and African player of the year George Weah ran for election as president of Liberia ten years later. He lost to Ellen Johnson-Sirleaf.

Fox in the box

A fox had a brush with soccer fame when it appeared during a Glasgow Rangers versus Celtic game in 1996. It gave several players the slip before dashing into the crowd and leaving no clue as to how it had got in.

Tarnished legends

The reputations of two of England's most respected post-war legends took a massive knock when 60-year-old classified National Archives were opened in 2009. Sir Stanley Matthews and his England and Blackpool team-mate Stan Mortensen were unmasked as black marketeers during World War 2. In 1945, although still serving RAF personnel, they were part of an FA Services team playing an exhibition match in newly liberated Belgium. They were caught trying to sell coffee and soap on the black market, were investigated by RAF police and given a dressing down by their commanding officer on charges of "conduct prejudicial to good order and discipline".

Player's smoking prank bombs

A player who let off a smoke grenade in his team's dressing room was sacked in 2012. Twenty-one-year-old reserve team midfielder Jacob Mellis, who was rated as a possible star of the future at Chelsea, was fired for the incident which triggered a fire alarm and a full evacuation. Another starlet, Billy Clifford, 19, was fined after bringing the grenade to the club's training ground.

Scaling up for success

A goldfish is one of the more unusual football club mascots – except if you are a fan of Carlisle United. In floods in the area in 2005 a goldfish washed from its domestic tank wound up floundering on the club's Brunton Park pitch. It was rescued by Emma Story, the daughter of the club owner, Fred, and she christened the fish Judy. The club won their next game and fans began to say the fish represented the fighting spirit of the club. Judy took up residence as the club's mascot and has presided from her bowl in the club's reception over a rise from non-league obscurity to League One.

Gyula is forever No. 1

An old footballer's dream finally came truly when he signed for the club of his dreams in 2008. Legendary Hungarian goalkeeper Gyula Grosics had wanted to sign for Ferencvaros in the 1960s but was refused permission by the communist regime running the country at the time. In 2008 that wrong was at least partially righted when the club "signed" the 82-year-old. He was invited to kick off and then stand in goal for a few minutes in a friendly against Sheffield United, then Ferencvaros retired his No. 1 shirt. The 1954 World Cup runner-up who was known as the Black Panther, technically remains a player for the club. He developed the "sweeper-keeper" style in which goalkeepers came out to act as an extra defender.

Model professional?

Frenchman David Ginola swapped his wing position with Paris St Germain for modelling in 1992. He signed a contract with designer Nino Cerruti and reckoned the catwalk was more daunting than any soccer crowd.

De Burgh comes to aid of sick Babbel

When Liverpool star Markus Babbel was diagnosed with crippling Guillan-Barré Syndrome help was offered in 2001 from an unusual source – Chris de Burgh. The Irish singer-songwriter wanted to attempt to heal the defender's leg paralysis with "positive energy". De Burgh visited Babbel in a German hospital and the player was apparently surprised when de Burgh opened his bag and brought out a large crystal lamp "to create a better atmosphere in the room and support your well-being", de Burgh told him. He then closed his eyes and stroked Babbel's paralysed legs, and the player said he could actually feel some warmth in his limbs. However, there was no miraculous recovery because de Burgh said Babbel needed "longer, more intense treatment".

£65,000 was the price of cigar attack

A player who stubbed a cigar into the eye of a team-mate was ordered to pay £65,000 in compensation to his victim. Newcastle United's bad-boy midfielder Joey Barton agreed the out-of-court settlement in 2009 with former Manchester City colleague Jamie Tandy. The 2004 incident happened at a Christmas party in a nightclub and Tandy's sight was saved although he was scarred for life. By 2009 he had left football and, after a bout of alcoholism, was working as a window cleaner. Barton, who has served a jail term for off-the-field violence offences, did not admit liability.

Player cheats death

A player who collapsed on the pitch when his heart stopped was "dead" for 78 minutes. It took medics more than an hour – and 15 defibrillator shocks – to get Fabrice Muamba's heart beating normally again. The Bolton Wanderers' midfielder suddenly collapsed during an FA Cup fifth round tie in March 2012. The match was abandoned as a frantic battle to save the 23-year-old England international prospect was carried out on Tottenham Hotspur's White Hart Lane pitch and continued in an ambulance. Muamba was in intensive care at a London hospital for some days before he recovered consciousness. A player through and through, he soon asked medics, "Did we lose? Why did they stop the game?"

Injured – in bed?

His own bed proved dangerous for Reading striker Leroy Lita in 2007. He had to have a spell in the treatment room after an early morning stretch in bed saw him pull a leg muscle.

Dennis is no winger

Dutch player Dennis Bergkamp developed a fear of flying and never stepped on a plane again after a 1994 bomb scare. He was with the Dutch World Cup squad on an internal flight in the US when the scare occurred.

Free kick hat-trick

Serbian Sinisa Mihajlovic scored a hat-trick of free kicks as Lazio beat his former club Sampdoria 5–2 during a 1998 Italian Serie A league match.

Mario barred from prison

Manchester City's eccentric striker Mario Balotelli once visited a women's prison. Bored on his day off and with a relative's child to entertain, the Italian drove to the prison near Brescia in Italy. He was allowed to go after questioning in which he explained away his bizarre behavior with a characteristic shrug and the claim that he was "specially curious that it was a prison for women".

Sexploits meant early bath for Mal

Malcolm Allison's "sexploits" were in the news in the 1960s and 1970s as much as his successes with clubs such as Manchester City and Crystal Palace. Rarely without his trademark fedora hat, he enjoyed the Manchester club scene of the era with drinking pals such as George Best. He lost his job at London club Crystal Palace after allowing porn actress Fiona Richmond to join the team in the post-match bath. He "escorted" Christine Keeler of Profumo affair fame and singer Dorothy Squires as well as string of Bunny Girls, one of whom he married.

Fab timing

Liverpool defender Fabio Aurelio missed the start of the 2011–12 Premier League season after he twisted his knee playing beach games with his children.

Thumped by a mike

Legendary Brazilian striker Ronaldo was left with a black eye after being struck by a microphone during a media scrum following his debut for Corinthians in 2009.

Incredible shrinking goal

Kim Christensen was spotted making his goal smaller in 2009 by kicking the posts inwards. The Danish goalkeeper, who plays his football in Sweden for Gothenburg, had some explaining to do for making the moveable goals smaller, but defiantly admitted it was not the first time he, or other goalkeepers, had used the tactic to increase their odds in a match. He said: "I got the tip from a goalkeeper friend a few years ago and I've done it ever since from time to time." The Swedish FA took no action against Christensen.

Fans watch parachute display horror

Thousands of fans watched as a matchday parachute stunt went horribly wrong in 1998. RAF parachutist Nigel Rogoff was part of a demonstration, but instead of landing on the Aston Villa pitch he struck the Trinity Street stand and plunged 100 feet to the ground. Severely injured, Rogoff needed a life-saving 177 pints of blood but still lost a leg. Later at a rehabilitation centre he found love with one of his nurses, married and produced twins.

High-handed

When in 1995 FIFA banned matches being played at altitudes over 3,000 metres above sea level, the only country affected was Bolivia. Its capital La Paz is at 3,600 metres.

Headhunters jailed

Leaders of a notorious gang who had sparked a wave of football violence across England were jailed for a total of 38 years in 1987. The actions of the so-called "Chelsea Headhunters" were stopped by police infiltrating their ranks.

Grey area

Manchester United have never played in their grey away kit since 1996. With his team heading for a fifth straight defeat wearing the grey, coach Alex Ferguson made his team change to blue and white stripes at half-time – but still lost 3–1 to Southampton.

Defying physics

Brazilian Roberto Carlos hit the "impossible" free kick in 1997 against France. After an unusually long run-up, he struck the ball with the outside of his left foot. It veered right around the French wall and, just as it looked destined to go out of play, it swerved back towards the goal and in off a post.

Positive thinking penalties

Missing a penalty kick is all in the mind according to a sports psychologists' 2012 report. Players have to think big when stepping up to the spot, they said, because an optical illusion often makes the goal seem smaller. The Indiana research group also found that the goal looked smaller on psychological bad days and bigger on good ones. They recommended players should trick themselves into thinking the target was bigger.

Belly good

Fluminese won the Rio State Championship in 1995 when striker Renato Gaucho scored the winner over Flamengo by sticking out his stomach and diverting the ball into the net.

Home defeat

Chelsea's financial pursuit of former player Adrian Mutu was in its ninth year when the Premiership club won a 2012 judgment to assume ownership of three homes owned by the Romanian striker. The Mutu saga began in 2004 when the £15.8m player was banned from playing and sacked by his club after testing positive for cocaine. World football chiefs ordered Mutu to pay Chelsea £14m in compensation, but six years later the club was still pursuing the player through the courts when a US court granted it permission to seize the three homes valued at almost £3.5m.

Freedom for Jack

Englishman Jack Charlton was given the freedom of the city of Dublin for coaching the Republic of Ireland to the finals of Euro 88 and the World Cups of 1990 and 1994. In the 63 years prior Ireland had never qualified for a major tournament.

Blond ambition

The whole Romania team celebrated qualification for the second round of the 1998 World Cup finals by dyeing their hair blond for their final group game against Tunisia. The only exception was goalkeeper Bogdan Stelea, who was bald.

Pushy player

Italian striker Paolo Di Canio was banned for 11 games and fined £10,000 in 1998 for pushing over referee Paul Alcock in an English Premier League match. Volatile Di Canio had already been red-carded and never again played for his club Sheffield Wednesday.

Injunction fails to protect

England's Premier League was awash with speculation in 2001 about a high-profile player who was conducting not one, but two, extra-marital affairs. The player beat the media to the drop by securing an injunction against being exposed. The newspaper with the juicy details ready to print about the player, the lap dancer and the nursery nurse was the Sunday People and although it was gagged it ran the expose without names. Ultimately injunctions expire and when it did Garry Flitcroft, the captain of Blackburn Rovers, was the Lothario revealed and it had cost him around £200,000 in legal costs.

Bartram misses the game

Charlton Athletic goalkeeper Sam Bartram didn't have the foggiest idea what was happening when thick fog blanketed a 1956 league match against fellow Londoners Chelsea. Bartram stood for 20 minutes on his line peering into the murk but with little action coming his way. Then a figure emerged from the fog, a policeman who explained that the game had been called off some time before and the teams and the big crowd had all gone home.

Shirt charity

One of the most seen footballs shirts in Afghanistan today is not Manchester United or Real Madrid but that of English club Bradford City. The struggling club responded to an appeal for football shirts for Afghanistan's new league and sent 2,400.

Pranksters play feng shui trick

So-called feng shui experts called in by Bristol Rovers in 1999 seemed to have all the answers. They placed a ceramic frog in the stadium entrance, potted plants in the dressing room and a tank of toy fish behind a goal in a bid to change the club's fortunes. The "experts" then unmasked themselves as hoaxers on a TV show called Gatecrashers. Incredibly, the fake feng shui seemed to work as, after the initial hiccup of a defeat, the club went all the way to the play-offs the next season.

Superfan Paul

Ardent fan of English lower league club Luton Town, Paul Goodwin, jetted from Majorca in 2001 to watch his team win a Worthington Cup tie 2–1 and flew back the following day. The return flight cost him £100, but he had won £500 from a bet on the result.

Renton who?

A village team lays claim to being the first soccer "world champions". Scottish Cup holders Renton from Dumbartonshire won the unofficial title in a cross-border game in 1888 when they beat English FA Cup winners West Bromwich 4–1 to be acclaimed "champions of the United Kingdom and the world".

Herr wee go

German goalkeeper Jens Lehmann couldn't find privacy when he needed to pee during a 2009 Champions League match and had to go in front of 36,000 Stuttgart fans. The stopper jumped the advertising hoardings, bobbed down to wee and then ran back on the pitch to thwart an attack by Romanian visitors Unirea Urziceni.

Le Pen rant

French far-right National Front leader Jean-Marie Le Pen marked France's 1998 World Cup win with criticism about the victors' ethnic make-up. He said having black, white and Arab players meant the team did not look "sufficiently French".

The George Weah cousin hoax

A "phone call" from the 1996 World Player of the Year George Weah got Southampton excited about the prospect of his "cousin" Ali Dia, who was available for a trial. By coincidence manager Graeme Souness had a massive injury crisis and he put Dia on as a substitute. After a few minutes of completely inept play the substitute was substituted and it became clear that it hadn't been Weah on the phone, and Dia was not Weah's cousin. Dia could not even hold down a place at non-league Gateshead to where he was later shipped and then released completely.

Pallet-able

Wooden pallets were used as the base of a grass pitch at a 1994 World Cup game between the USA and Switzerland. The match at Detriot's Silverdome was the first World Cup game staged indoors.

I spy

George Best once revealed the secret life of a team-mate who got his kicks through voyeurism. The player Best called "The Ferret" used to hide in hotel closets hoping to catch a glimpse of team-mates' sexual encounters.

Mutu drug bill

Adrian Mutu was ordered in 2009 to pay Chelsea £14.65m after losing his appeal against a FIFA ruling for a breach of contract. The striker, who cost the Blues £15m in 2003, was sacked and given a seven-month worldwide football ban a year later after testing positive for cocaine. FIFA had ruled on the level of compensation in 2008 but Mutu appealed, describing the judgment as "inhumane and unjust". A Court of Arbitration for Sport also ruled against Romanian-born Mutu. The compensation figure for Chelsea, based on lost earnings, was calculated on the length of time Mutu's contract had left to run, and was the highest-ever handed down by FIFA.

Cameras capture moment of madness

Welsh striker John Hartson was unlucky to have had a TV crew at West Ham's training ground to record a bust-up in which he kicked a team-mate in the head. The film was seen globally within hours after volatile Hartson planted his boot into Eyal Berkovic's head in 1998. Former Arsenal striker Hartson claimed he lashed out after the Israeli midfielder had punched Hartson in the leg as he attempted to help Berkovic to his feet. Hartson, who admitted in his biography that this was an error of judgement, was fined for the incident.

Bribery claim

A referee claimed a club attempted to bribe him with prostitutes before an cup match in 2000. The club claimed the women involved were "folk singers".

The short life of wild man Friday

English league player Robin Friday knew his own failings and entitled his biography *The Greatest Footballer You Never Saw*. Friday's wild streak and a penchant for drink and drugs meant he never fulfilled his footballing potential although he was a prolific scorer for Reading. His drinking was legendary and early in his career his team, Hayes, started a match with only ten players, as Friday was finishing a pint in the local pub. When Cardiff City boss Jimmy Andrews enquired why he had secured Friday for a cut-price £30,000 from Reading he was reportedly told: "You'll see." Friday was arrested for fare dodging as he arrived in Cardiff by train! Friday died of a heart attack aged 38 in 1990.

Cup-winning cups

American Brandi Chastain celebrated the winning of the 1999 Women's World Cup by removing her shirt and revealing her sports bra.

Hat-trick of misses

Argentinian striker Martin Palermo missed a penalty three times in a Copa America match against Colombia in 1999. He hit the crossbar and blasted the second over, only for the goalkeeper to save the third. Argentina lost 3–0.

Donna is boss for a day

Donna Powell became the first female manager in the English semi-professional men's game – for 24 hours. In 2009 she took over struggling Fisher Athletic of the Conference South league for one match as a thank you for her fundraising efforts. Although the coach of a very successful boy's under-11 side, she could not weave the same magic in her short tenure with Fisher, who lost 2–1 to Eastleigh. Her one-day appointment caused a row among those who were against females in football but she had been working on the turnstiles at Fisher and had raised £500 for the struggling club.

Helmet hell

Rocks and bottles were flying on to the field from the restive terraces, but the referee drew the line when he saw a linesman felled by a motorcycle helmet. The 1996 Argentinian league match between Penarol and Danubio turned ugly when Penarol fans got upset at the fact that their team was down 1–0 and with only a few minutes remaining. They bombarded the pitch with all sorts of objects, but the match was suspended at the sight of the linesman unconscious on the grass with the motorcycle helmet that had just hit him lying nearby.

Police blockade

Argentinian fans crossing the River Plate in boats to get to the 1930 World Cup final in Montevideo were met by Uruguayan police and relieved of firearms.

Public attack on girlfriend

Aston Villa and England striker Stan Collymore had a high-profile row in a crowded Paris bar that ended with him attacking his girlfriend. TV personality Ulrika Jonsson had been in the Auld Alliance bar with Glasgow Rangers star Ally McCoist when Collymore demanded that she leave with him. In the argument he allegedly dragged her to the floor and aimed kicks at her head. Collymore later publicly apologised, citing "jealousy and drink" as reasons. He added: "In a fit of petulant temper I struck out at the girl I love and immediately regretted my actions, but by then it was too late."

Painkiller was a pain

A bid to minimize an injury to Manchester City striker Sergio Aguero badly backfired and he missed several vital Premiership matches in March 2012. A painkilling spray applied to an ankle injury caused an unforeseen reaction, leaving Aguero's foot swollen and blistered. The player was on the sidelines as City lost their grip on the league leadership but he returned in time to score the goal that clinched the title.

No love

Animosity between two German clubs was so intense that players from Nuremberg and Furth selected for the national team travelled separately by train to play against Holland in 1924. When Auer scored the only – and winning – goal, only Furth colleagues celebrated with him. The Nuremberg players ignored him.

Having a trial – in court

Two high-profile players of the successful Leeds United side at the turn of the 21st century went on trial in 2001 over an attack on an Asian student. It followed a nightclub incident that left Safraz Najeib severely injured. Midfielder Lee Bowyer and defender Jonathan Woodgate were charged with causing grievous bodily harm with intent and affray. Bowyer was cleared, while Woodgate was convicted of affray and sentenced to community service. In 2005, Bowyer, who was suspended for cannabis use in 1995, agreed a £170,000 out-of-court settlement with the victim and his less seriously injured brother.

Eriberto confesses to name change

Brazilian footballer Eriberto confessed in 2007 that he wasn't himself and was suspended by FIFA for playing under a false name. The Chievo midfielder admitted he had changed his identity to help his career by making teams believe he was younger. The former Palmeiras and Bologna player was really Luciano Siqueira de Oliveira and four years older than the 27 he claimed to be at the time of his revelation. He had previously been listed as Eriberto Silva da Conceicao, born in Rio de Janiero in 1979.

Part-timers slaughtered

Luxembourg side Jeunesse Hautcharage crashed to a then-record aggregate score of 21–0 in the 1971–72 European Cup Winners' Cup. In the side of part-timers against Chelsea were a one-armed man and another whose glasses were held on by an elastic band.

Messi-ing about

Superstar Lionel Messi was bizarrely accused of being a messenger for Syrian rebels – by the way he moved his body during a televised match. The Barcelona player was dragged into a weird propaganda war as Syria collapsed into civil strife in 2012. The Argentinian striker's performance was one of the highlights of a Spanish League game against Real Madrid beamed to pro-President Assad Syrian TV channel Addounia. A commentator claimed in an online video that Messi's darting runs were a secret code for gun runners helping the rebels in the Syrian conflict. He alleged that by tracking the direction of Messi's dribbles, passes and shots it was possible to draw a route into Syria. The voiceover said that Messi's initial run denoted arms being loaded in Lebanon and that a pass showed the arms going through the rebel stronghold of Homs. Then, as Messi's teammate Pedro scored, the mystery voice translated this as the arms going by bus to their final destination.

President sheikhs them up

Chaos reigned at the 1982 World Cup finals when the president of the Kuwait FA, Sheikh Fahid Al-Ahmad Al-Sabah, marched on to the field to berate a referee and threatened to take his side off. The row was over Kuwait, trailing 3–1 to Michel Platini's France, conceding a fourth goal scored by Alain Giresse because several of their players had stopped, thinking that they had heard the ref's whistle. Incredibly, the referee gave in to Al-Sabah's forceful argument and the goal was ruled out. In the remaining minutes France did go on to add a fourth goal and the referee would lose his international status, presumably for being weak.

God squad

Faith healer Eileen Drewery was brought into the England squad as an advisor prior to the 1998 World Cup. A long-time friend and mentor of coach Glenn Hoddle, he said she was "more of an agony aunt".

Fatal love

The love of football led to the death of legendary Arsenal manager Herbert Chapman in 1934. Despite having a bad cold, he insisted on attending an inconsequential Arsenal reserve match and days later was dead from pneumonia.

Playing with a gun at their heads

Zaire played in the 1974 World Cup in West Germany literally with a gun to their heads. The surprise first black-African qualifiers had been warned by the country's then President Mobutu Sese Seko that should they lose by four goals or more to holders Brazil in their final group match, there would be dire consequences. They only lost by three goals and the team returned home unscathed. But the enormous pressure showed with a bizarre incident. As the Brazilians prepared to take a free kick 25 yards from his goal, Zaire's defender Mwepu Ilunga burst from the defensive wall and simply hoofed the ball upfield. It landed him with a yellow card.

Armed and dangerous

Uruguayan Hector Castro remains the only one-armed man to score a World Cup final goal. In 1930 the forward who had lost his right forearm in an electric saw accident aged 13, helped his country to a 4–2 win over Argentina.

Disappearing goal

The mystery of the goal that wasn't is still a talking point with Dundee United fans in Scotland. During a 1993 game with Partick Thistle, United scored a goal through Paddy Connolly, who blasted home from close range. As the ball bounced back out of the goal, it was caught by a defender who handed it to keeper Andy Murdoch to send upfield for the restart. Unbelievably, neither the referee nor his linesmen spotted the goal or the handball and waved play on. The ref dismissed the protests of livid Dundee players, who had the last laugh by winning anyway.

Team trapped

The great Honved team were destroyed by the Hungarian uprising of 1956. The side, which included such great names as Puskas, Kocsis and Czibor, were trapped in Spain when the Russian tanks rolled into Hungary. Some players never returned to their homeland.

Ball boy's balls-up

A ball boy got himself on the score sheet in a Brazilian league game between Atletico Sorocaba and Santacruzense in 2006. With Sorocaba leading by a goal in the dying minutes, a Santacruzense chance zipped past the post. An unknown but cheeky ball boy brought the ball back to the pitch, then impishly sidefooted it into the goal where Brazil's first top-level woman referee Silvia Regina de Oliveira saw it and assumed that the shot she thought she had seen go wide, had actually gone in. The game finished 1–1 and the Brazilian FA were forced to uphold the result, but the referee and her linesman were suspended.

Miss Ross misses

The USA was determined to pile on the razzmatazz for the opening ceremony of the 1994 World Cup finals and spectacular it was – apart from singer Diana Ross' footwork. At the outlandishly glitzy opening in Chicago's Soldier Field Stadium, all the Supremes singer had to do was sing a song before burying a close-range penalty past a goalkeeper paid to let it go into a goal that would split in two. MC Oprah Winfrey had already fallen off the dais during her presentation and Ross, who had never kicked a ball of any shape, shanked her shot to the left of the target. But the goal still snapped in two, releasing a thousand white balloons and tons of glitter.

My name is Sh...Sh...Sh...Shmolik

One of Belarus' finest referees did not have his finest hour and a half at a Premier League match between Vitebsk and Naftan. International ref Sergei Shmolik, according to eye-witnesses, spent much of the game staggering around the centre circle, failing to keep up with play and refusing to issue any cards despite some heavy tackles flying about. At the end of the game, Shmolik was helped off the pitch by another official, waving to the crowd as he left. Tests revealed huge levels of alcohol in his system and the Belarus FA suspended Shmolik, who claimed that his strange performance was due to "a bad back".

Keeper scores

The 1967–68 season in England opened with a sensation when a goalkeeper scored the first goal. Pat Jennings of Tottenham Hotspur succeeded with an 80-yard, wind-assisted punt in the FA Charity Shield. Cup winners Spurs drew 3–3 with league champions Manchester United.

Sweet success

Barcelona's world-renowned club was formed by sugar trader Hans Kamper who was visiting his uncle in the city. He liked it so much he stayed, changed his name to Joan and started the football club in 1898 with local players reinforced by British and Swiss ex-patriots.

I'm off

Sectarian death threats sparked the end of Northern Ireland star Neil Lennon's international career. The Catholic midfielder had upset loyalists by saying he wanted a united Irish team.

Spot the spot competition

A referee had trouble hitting the spot when he awarded a penalty in a 1977 English First Division game between Derby County and Manchester City. The trouble was he couldn't find the spot for a spot kick because, being late in the season, the grass had been worn away. City goalkeeper Joe Corrigan's attempt to help by pacing out 12 yards got him a yellow card, so the solution was to paint a new spot. County groundsman Bob Smith got to work with tape measure and bucket of white paint on a nice white spot before Gerry Daly buried the ball in the net for Derby.

Net result

After watching a dispute over whether a ball had crossed the goal line, university professor John Brodie went home and designed the first "net pocket" and saw them used in an 1891 English league match.

Games promotion winner gets Harry

One of the English Premier League's top managers was the prize in a computer game promotion in 2009–10. Harry Redknapp, the boss of Tottenham Hotspur at the time, was to be available on the end of a phone line 24/7 to dispense advice on all aspects of football. In a Willy Wonka-style offer, a lucky ticket was hidden in a copy of the Football Manager 2010 game, and it contained Redknapp's private phone number. Redknapp, a coach with a reputation for turning around ailing teams, said: "I've got plenty of years experience in football management so hopefully I'll be able to pass on some valuable words of wisdom."

Concrete evidence of practical "joke"

So-called performance artists laid a nasty trap for any half-cut football fan that had been indulging in Germany's beer at the 2006 World Cup. They filled leather footballs with concrete and left them invitingly around Berlin with a sign in English "Can u kick it?". What football fan worth his salt could resist such an invitation? Several didn't and ended up in hospital with foot injuries. Police arrested several people, thought to be a group of Austrian artists.

A concrete balls-up

The installation of a giant concrete ball made for a stadium to be used in the 2010 World Cup finals seemed jinxed. The ball was airlifted to the Johannesburg stadium by helicopter in 2009 and was just about to be lowered on to the mountings above the main entrance when engineers discovered the brackets were wrongly placed. It was decided to return the concrete monstrosity to the workshops by truck but journey planners failed to take a low bridge into account. It smashed the bridge to the ground, causing traffic chaos.

Buggy-ed

Swansea City's Alan Tate lost six months of his career due to a bizarre golfing accident – just as his club reached the Premiership for the first time. The 28-year-old defender was a passenger in a golf buggy that spun out of control. In the crash he fractured the tibia of his left leg.

Newcastle players take a battering

Civil war broke out amid the Newcastle United ranks during a 2005 Premiership match against Aston Villa. After Villa went 3–0 up, tempers flared between midfielders Kieron Dyer and Lee Bowyer and they started punching each other. The warring duo were not separated by their own team-mates but by opposition player Gareth Barry. Bowyer's shirt was ripped in the fracas and both were sent off. The warring pair later sheepishly appeared at a press conference to say how much they regretted their punch-up.

Iran football fans vote against TV ban

The Iranian Football Federation (FFI) clashed with fans in 2009 over the possible banning of one of the country's top TV football programmes – and lost a ballot by text message. Adel Ferdosipour, the country's most famous football commentator and presenter of the programme Navad (90), faced being blacked out because of his on-air criticism of the federation's efficiency. Ferdosipour even dared to conduct a text survey of viewers asking whether people were in favour of or against the programme and won a 97 per cent vote in favour. More than two million people sent messages. FFI is affiliated to the government sports organisation and run by a deputy of President Mahmoud Ahmadinejad.

Jose is spot on

Paraguyan goalkeeper Jose Luis Chilavert became the first goalkeeper to score a hat-trick. The seasoned penalty taker scored three times from the spot as his Argentinian league side Velez Sarsfield won 6–1 in 1999.

In the pink

Italian club Juventus played the first six years of their existence in a nice feminine pink. It was only in 1903, when the pink faded, that the Bianconeri adopted the now-famous black and white vertical stripes based on England's Notts County club.

Kiss and run

Walter Zenga dashed to the touchline to kiss his girlfriend in celebration when his Major League Soccer side New England Revolution scored in 1997. He was still dashing back when the opposition kicked off and aimed a shot from 55 yards towards Zenga's net. He didn't make it but neither did the shot.

Lambert's rampage is an internet hit

Millions of internet hits were recorded on a video of an American woman's violent rampage during a match in New Mexico. Elizabeth Lambert, 20, was playing for the University of New Mexico against Brigham Young University in the 2009 semi-finals of the Mountain West Conference when she was caught on camera punching one player in the back, pulling another to the ground by her hair and kicking out at several others. Lambert later apologised saying: "I let my emotions get the best of me in a heated situation. I take full responsibility." However, Lambert also attracted a number of admirers, with a Facebook group called "Go Elizabeth Lambert" claiming over 3,000 fans.

McCall and Myers in Bradford spat

When a team are 6–1 down, players need to pull together and summon up the fighting spirit. That is sort of what Bradford City's Stuart McCall and Andy Myers did in 2001 when the supposed team-mates came to blows during the Bantams' thrashing at the hands of Leeds United. Bradford captain McCall had to have stitches in a facial wound after Myers struck him just before half-time, then the smaller McCall seemed to aim a headbutt at the central defender, but fortunately it missed.

Custom-ary beating

England player Kevin Keegan was beaten by airport customs men for sitting on a luggage carousel at Belgrade in the former Yugoslavia. After his release, sporting a bloodied nose, he proceeded to get his revenge by scoring for England.

King of the game

Stanley Matthews was given the official title of "King of Football" by a Ghanaian tribe in 1957. The jet-heeled winger who played for Blackpool and England was later also knighted in his own country.

Record record

"Back Home", the 1970 World Cup song recorded by England's squad, became the first football song to top Britain's pop charts.

Fan arrested for mascot attack

A 15-year-old Burton Albion fan was arrested for punching one of the club's mascots during a 2010 game his team won. The attack was on Bettie Brewer – the female partner of male mascot Billy. The cartoon-type character, which was wearing the newly promoted League Two side's team colours, suffered minor injuries during the attack. Stewards dashed on to the pitch to stop the attack and held the suspect.

Poor value

Ajax smuggled Froylan Ledezma Stevens from under the nose of bitter rivals Feyenoord in 1997. As the 19-year-old arrived at Amsterdam airport, Ajax agents pounced and took him out a side door. The ruse backfired because, although Ajax signed him for £4.5m, they played him just twice before he returned to his native Costa Rica.

Mourinho kidnap plot foiled

Police in Italy believed they foiled a plot to kidnap and ransom Inter Milan coach Jose Mourinho in 2010. Four members of a Macedonian gang were arrested after police found evidence that the movements of Mourinho and his family were being closely monitored. It was believed a gang specialising in taking celebrity hostages was planning an operation at Mourinho's Lake Como home. In an undercover operation police found photographs and video footage of the coach, his wife and their two children. Mourinho, the self-styled "Special One", was high profile for his managerial style and his outspoken comments. His security had to be beefed up in 2009 when his comments about Ramadan affecting a player's performance sparked Muslim death threats.

Strikers strike out – at each other

Charlton Athletic's twin strike force were a formidable team until an on-pitch difference of opinion split them. Derek Hales and Mike Flanagan were sent off for brawling during an FA Cup third-round tie against lower-league side Maidstone at The Valley in 1979. The problem came with five minutes to go and the game level at 1–1, over a ball played through to Hales by Flanagan. Hales was ruled offside and furiously told Flanagan in no uncertain terms that he had wanted the ball played a lot earlier. The riposte by Flanagan, who had scored Charlton's equaliser minutes earlier, which got tempers flaring was that he had been doing that all season but Hales had been too slow to take advantage.

Grobbelaar bawls out youngster

Liverpool team-mates Steve McManaman and Bruce Grobbelaar famously fell out during a 1993 Merseyside derby that left midfielder McManaman feeling choked. Goalkeeper Grobbelaar, always a vocal presence in his penalty area, was indignant when McManaman hit a weak clearance that gifted Everton the lead and told him what he thought in no uncertain terms. Macca, one of the group of cheeky young stars at the club, yelled back at the keeper. The 6-foot 1-inch, well-built Grobbelaar grabbed his slighter-built team-mate by the throat and pushed him away. McManaman wisely decided that enough was enough and walked away from the confrontation.

Not white

Hertha Berlin star Bartosz Karwan was fined after it was found he was not wearing a team shirt – just as he was going on as a substitute in 2003. Only wearing a plain white t-shirt the Pole was ordered back to the bench by incensed coachHuub Stevens.

Racists disqualified

South Africa were thrown out of the inaugural Africa Cup of Nations in 1957 for refusing to play a multiracial team. Proposed opponents Ethiopia were given a bye to the next round and reached the final.

Half-time scrap with colleague

An argument between team-mates was not just a quick, passing thing. The pair started arguing during the first half of a 2000 game and carried on their disagreement into the dressing room and through half-time. It was verbal until they came to the dressing room where the pair of strikers actually came to blows. It ended when one player refused to come out for the second half. It can't have been big-match tension that got the pair so worked up because the incident was at a reserve team match in front of a sparse crowd.

Southall's sit-down protest

Everton keeper Neville Southall stayed in his goal for the whole of a match at Goodison Park in 1990 – including during the half-time break. The first match of a new season opened with hope and expectation until Everton went 3–0 down. After his miserable first half against newly promoted Leeds United, Wales international Southall refused to join the rest of his team-mates in the changing rooms at half-time. Instead, he propped himself up against a post and sat disconsolately for the entire duration of the interval. His sit-down protest almost worked as Everton rallied and, although they lost, the score was only 3–2.

Off day

Chart-topping singer Robbie Williams was dismissed for dissent while guesting for his beloved Port Vale in a testimonial against Aston Villa.

Biting tackle

Player Rannord Jones was charged with assault and terroristic threatening in Newark, Delaware after allegedly biting on the chin the referee who gave him a red card in 2008.

Goalie sues daughter in trophy row

A struggling law student was left with a £6,000 legal bill in 2007 because her football legend father sued her for the return of his trophies. Ex-Everton and Wales goalie Neville Southall gave his FA Cup medal, his MBE and a number of international caps to daughter Samantha when she was ten. But nine years later after splitting from Samantha's mother, Southall told a court he never intended for his daughter to keep the trophy collection worth £55,000. The teenager sobbed as a judge at Liverpool's civil and family court ordered her to return the memorabilia to her father and pay £6,000 costs. The law student said: "I am devastated – I idolised my dad. I don't know how I'll pay."

Loyalty plea

Italian midfielder Benito Carbone was adamant about his commitment to unfashionable Bradford City in 2002 – well almost. On 2 February he said: "I love Bradford; I signed for four years and I want to stay." On 4 February he added: "There's no problem to play here for two years." On 6 February he moved to Middlesbrough.

Superman Ireland shows credentials

Manchester City midfielder Stephen Ireland had no phone box to change in, so he dropped his shorts to reveal the inspiration for his winning goal in a 2007 match – his Superman underpants. After volleying City to a 1–0 win over Sunderland at the Eastlands Stadium he revealed to laughing fans blue underpants with a Superman logo. Even the English FA saw the funny side and took no disciplinary action, although an official said: "We will be reminding him of his responsibilities."

Cahill's goal celebration dedication

There was an outcry in 2008 when Australian striker Tim Cahill dedicated a goal to a brother who had been jailed for partially blinding a man. Millions watching on TV were puzzled when Everton's Cahill celebrated a goal by putting his wrists together as though handcuffed. He explained it was a gesture of support for his brother, who is serving a six-year sentence for grievous bodily harm. Tim said: "I am just proud that he is happy and I am happy and I'm thinking of him always." However, his words glossed over what was described in court as "a vicious and cowardly attack" in which the victim lost the sight in one eye.

Stand-in's brilliance proved fatal

Being multi-talented in several positions in his team proved fatal for ace winger Libardo Zuniga. He swapped the freedom on the wing in 1977 for the goalmouth when Colombian second division side Santa Rose de Cabal's goalkeeper was injured. After taking over in goal Zuniga literally threw himself into the new task and played a blinder. Unfortunately for Zuniga, his performance was so good that it upset an opposition striker, who vented his frustration by kicking the stand-in goalie in the groin with such force that he subsequently died from the injuries.

Slumbered and lumbered

SV Hamburg's Yugoslav coach Branko Zebec developed a reputation for sleeping during matches. He won the Bundesliga in 1978 and was runner-up a year later but was fired in 1980.

Souness flag joy causes fury

Graeme Souness committed one of the cardinal sins of Turkish football in 1996. As a celebration for his Galatasaray team's surprise Turkish Cup win over bitter local Istanbul rivals Fenerbahce he planted a Galatasaray flag in the middle of the Fenerbahce pitch. It sparked fury because, before the game, the clubs had traded a insults. The Fenerbahce chairman made comments about Souness as a coach and so, with his inflammatory flag celebration in the iconic style of Turkish hero Ulubatli Hasan who was killed as he planted the Ottoman flag at the end of the siege of Constantinople, he metaphorically stuffed the words back down their speaker's throat. Galatasaray won the first leg 1–0, then in the hellish atmosphere of the Fenerbahce Stadium, the teams were level on aggregate before an extra-time Dean Saunders' goal won it. Souness was never punished.

Foot in two camps

Enigmatic England striker Stan Bowles turned out for his country against Holland in 1977 sporting different boots. With an Adidas on his left foot and a Gola on his right, he was honouring two separate boot sponsorship deals.

Premature end

France, who took two weeks to sail to the 1930 World Cup in South America, were soon on the boat back when a referee blew for time six minutes early. The French had gone a goal down to Argentina in 81 minutes and were attacking when the whistle went on 84 minutes.

Old wounds opened

It took almost 40 years for France to play its old colony Algeria in an international. But the politically sensitive match in 2001, 39 years after Algeria's independence, had to be abandoned when thousands of youths rioted at the game in Paris.

Pleased as a parrot

The famous white cockerel is on the badge of Tottenham Hotspur, but it might well have been a parrot instead. The club made a ground-breaking tour of Argentina and Uruguay in 1908, a trip that took weeks by ship. On the return two Spurs players used pirate costumes and the ship's parrot to win a fancy dress competition. The parrot was presented to the club when the ship docked again in England and the bird took up residence at the White Hart Lane ground where, after a pampered 11 years as a mascot, it died.

Dress for success

Gary Neville, the former Manchester United regular, tried to lengthen his side's winning runs in the 1990s and Noughties by wearing the same clothes on matchdays, including belts and shoes.

Fury over Di Canio fascist salute

Lazio striker Paolo Di Canio defended the raised-arm salute that earned him a one-game Italian league ban in 2004 by saying: "I am a fascist, not a racist." Di Canio caused an outcry among politicians, players, fans and Jewish groups in a country desperate to forget its fascist past by making the stiff-armed salute after being substituted in the 1–1 draw with Juventus. The player, who was also fined €10,000, added: "I made the Roman salute because it's a salute from a comrade to his comrades and was meant for my people. I do not want to incite violence or racial hatred." Di Canio had made the gesture several times before during his time at Lazio, which has historically been linked with former dictator Mussolini.

Handcuff support for killer driver

Ipswich Town fined David Norris for a goal celebration in 2008 in support of a friend who killed two boys and maimed their father. Town docked Norris the maximum two weeks' wages for a controversial handcuffs' goal celebration in honour of goalkeeper Luke McCormick who was jailed for seven years and four months for killing Arron Peak, ten, and his brother Ben, eight, while drunkenly driving home from Norris' wedding on 7 June 2008. Ipswich acted promptly in punishing Norris whose fine went to a road safety charity. Norris, who apologised to the dead boys' parents, had insisted the gesture was a message to a friend who had "made a mistake".

Hristo almighty

Never modest, Bulgaria and Barcelona striker Hristo Stoichkov was quoted in 1990 as saying: "There are two Christs. One plays for Barcelona, the other is in heaven."

Goalkeeping can be a dangerous job

Throughout football history there have been numerous examples of goalkeeping proving fatal. Dumbarton's Joshua Wilkinson died from peritonitis two days after a hard collision in a match against Glasgow Rangers in 1921. Malaga's Jose Gallardo died from a brain haemorrhage in 1987, a month after receiving a head blow in a collision during a Spanish Second Division game against Vigo. In 1934 Charlton Athletic's keeper Alex Wright lost his life after demonstrating his match-winning saves from a recent game. Standing on top of a raft off Torre Abbey Sands in Torquay, he dived into shallow water and broke his neck on rocks. Wolverhampton Wanderers goalkeeper James Utterson died aged 21 from a kick to the heart he received during a reserve game in 1935.

Long wait

Vigili del Fuoco della Spezia had to wait 68 years to finally be recognised as the Italian league champions of 1943–44. Their win, including a victory over mighty Torino, was hampered by World War 2 raging in the country and their only Scudetto was not awarded until 2002.

Manic Maradona banned for drug use

If ever there was physical confirmation of the chaos in Diego Maradona's drug-fuelled personal life it was the picture of him maniacally staring into the camera while celebrating a goal at the 1994 World Cup finals staged in the USA. That crazed look was featured in the press the world over and might have been what led to him being picked for a drugs test, which he failed. He was sent home in disgrace for using ephedrine.

Kidnap plot

The kidnapping of Colombian Football Federation vice-president Hernan Campuzano almost led to the axing of the 2001 Copa America competition. When the threat to abandon it was announced Campuzano was freed and it went ahead.

Match probed

An investigation was launched after a team needing a nine-goal win to stand a chance of advancing through a World Cup qualification round recorded an amazing 10-0 victory. The Arab kingdom of Bahrain got lucky after just two minutes of the 2012 qualifier when Indonesia's goalkeeper was sent off. While there was no immediate proof of wrongdoing, an investigation was launched because the world governing body FIFA was trying to end the rumours of match-fixing influences of gambling syndicates. But in the end the massive 10-0 win didn't help Bahrain progress any further towards the 2014 World Cup finals as their main rival Qatar got the draw they needed to be Asian zone qualifier.

Not wanted in the hood

Manchester City's £24m star striker Mario Balotelli wasn't allowed to disguise himself in a hooded sweatshirt when he went shopping on a day off in 2012. The instantly-recognisable Italian player, who at the time sported a Mohican-style haircut, had his hood up in Manchester's Trafford centre but security guards told him that he needed to get out unless he was prepared to allow security cameras to see his face. The player left.

Cheers Ernie

The transfer fee for Ernie Blenkinsop's move to Hull City in 1921 was £100 and a barrel of beer. The left back went on to play for England 26 times.

Booger-ed off

Marco Boogers was a costly buy for West Ham United in 1995. His second game after a £1m transfer from Sparta Rotterdam earned him a red card, whereupon he disappeared, only turning up months later at a Dutch caravan park.

Getting waspish

Players for English Southern League side Abingdon United in 2003 blamed the club's new bright yellow strip for attracting wasps after players were stung.

On-field ear bashing

There was no comfortable half-time break in a warm dressing room for Hull City's under-performing team in December 2008. Manager Phil Brown kept them all on the field to deliver an on-field rollicking in full view of their travelling fans. Brown was furious that his side were 4–0 down at half-time in a Premier League match at Manchester City. He said: "I thought it was nice and cold and I thought I would keep the boys alive because they looked as if they were dead. I think 3,500 to 4,000 travelling fans deserved some kind of explanation for the first-half performance and it was difficult for me to do that from the confines of a changing room." Hull salvaged some pride by scoring a second-half goal and restricting City to just one more in a 5–1 scoreline.

Beer we go

Michael Schjonberg's reward for scoring the deciding goal that brought German team Hannover the 1992 DFB Cup was being able to drink as much beer as he wants in the city

Cameras catch out ref for first time

A century before similar evidence was available via video, movie cameras called a referee's decision into question. In the days before nets were used, and with Tottenham Hotspur leading the 1901 FA Cup final against Sheffield United 2–1, a ball that dropped wide of the Spurs post was given as a goal by referee Arthur Kingscott. By chance this was the first cup final captured by movie cameras and newsreels, which showed United had been lucky to get a draw through the "goal that never was". Spurs won the replay 3–1.

Commuting coach

Jurgen Klinsmann became a truly jet-age coach when he took over the German national team in 2004 – even though he lived in California, 6,000 miles from his homeland.

Referee ends the punishment

A referee cut short a game – because he felt sorry for the losing team. Marc Gevaert blew for time after just 86 minutes of a boys' league game in Belgium as FC Wijtschate trailed Vladslo 16–0. He revealed later that his fear was that the losing side was getting so collectively frustrated that someone might get sent off. After an hour Wijtschate were 11–0 down and some of their players begged the ref to end the slaughter. At 16–0 some Wijtschate players were so frustrated they started to kick the opposition and the ref feared serious injuries might occur.

Parking penalty

England captain John Terry apologised after leaving his Bentley in a disabled parking bay while he spent two hours over a meal at a restaurant near his Surrey home in 2008. He paid a £60 fine for the offence even though around the corner was a car park – charging 50p per hour.

Fair enough

Paolo Di Canio refused to score when Everton goalkeeper Paul Gerrard was injured attempting a clearance. West Ham's Di Canio caught the ball and stopped the game. He won a FIFA Fair Play Award.

Amy creates a first for women refs

An injury gave Amy Fearn the chance to become the first woman to referee a first-class league match in England. In 2009 she took charge for the final 20 minutes of Coventry's 1–0 home win over Nottingham Forest in the Coca-Cola Championship. Original referee Tony Bates had collapsed with a calf strain in the 71st minute and called assistant ref Fearn into action when he couldn't continue after treatment. Wendy Toms was the first female official in the Football League when she started as a fourth official in the early 1990s. Although Toms officiated games in the Premier League as an assistant referee she wasn't called upon to take over the whistle.

Jumbo pitch invasion

One of the more bizarre stoppages for a game was in 1979 when an elephant strolled into a Buckingham Town United Counties League match. The elephant's appearance was behind the referee's back and only the frantic waving of a goalkeeper alerted him to the intrusion. Minutes later two men appeared looking for an elephant that had gone walkabout from a travelling circus pitched nearby.

Chester match crippled by strikes

Strikes by players and a coach driver forced Chester City to cancel a game at Forest Green Rovers in England's Blue Square Premier League in 2010. Several players of cash-strapped Chester had refused to travel because they hadn't been paid, which meant the club, already rock bottom of the division with a 25-point deduction incurred for going into administration, were unable to raise a team of more than eight. The driver of the team coach also refused to move until the club paid the £675 for the journey in advance.

Not very Keane

Republic of Ireland captain Roy Keane quit the squad during the 2002 Japan/Korea World Cup finals after a furious bust-up with coach Mick McCarthy. It was reported he was unhappy with the training facilities for the squad on the island of Saipan.

Brolin claims a goal – 19 years late

Swedish striker Tomas Brolin was trying in 2010 to increase his goal tally for his country – 12 years after retirement. He wanted credit for a shot by team-mate Roland Nilsson, which deflected off Brolin's back into the net in a 2–1 win over Norway in 1991. Brolin, who played 47 times for his country, scoring 26 goals, said he had raised no objection to Nilsson getting the credit because he had never scored an international goal, but the defender then went on to score one more. Former Leeds, Parma and Crystal Palace striker Brolin applied to the Swedish FA to get the goal changed claiming in a TV interview that Nilsson "stole the goal".

Incredible sulk

Manchester United coach Sir Alex Ferguson has refused to talk to anyone from national broadcaster the BBC since the corporation showed a 2004 documentary questioning his professional relationship with football agent son Jason.

Who do voodoo?

Cameroon's goalkeeping coach Thomas Nkono was beaten, handcuffed and detained before an Africa Cup of Nations match with Mali in 2003 because he was suspected of leaving a voodoo charm on the pitch.

Berbatov kidnap drama

Manchester United's Dimitar Berbatov was the victim of a kidnapping as an up-and-coming young player in his native Bulgaria. The striker was abducted in 2000 aged 19 from the CSKA Sofia training ground by henchmen of a Bulgarian gangster. The idea was to force the emerging star to sign for the gangster's team. It needed tense negotiations and the intervention of Berbatov's father, himself a respected player in Bulgaria, to get the young Dimitar freed without harm. Berbatov later moved abroad to play for Bayer Leverkusen in Germany, and Tottenham and United in England.

Zorro mask fun at Charlton

Four thousand Charlton Athletic fans were issued with Zorro masks in 2003 to be used as a goal celebration. They were to be put on if their team scored against Fulham in an FA Cup fourth-round tie. The idea was a mickey-take of Fulham's Argentinian-born striker Facundo Sava whose own goal celebration was to pull on a mask from his sock every time he scored. The Zorro mask jape made for a fun atmosphere in the London derby but it backfired on Charlton because they didn't score in the game. Fulham, however, did – three times.

Surprise call-up

Out of the squad to play Liverpool in 1992, Arsenal midfielder Ray Parlour relaxed with several pints of beer in the hospitality lounge at Highbury, only to be told a substitute was injured and he was needed for the bench. A giddy Parlour's worst fears were realized when he was called into a game of which he remembered little.

Hospital charity can't beat the odds

It was a tall order for non-league side Farnborough Town in the 2003 FA Cup. No pressure – all they had to do was not only beat Premier League Arsenal, but also go on to win the cup for a charity to get £1m. Local newspaper proprietor and lifelong supporter Sir Ray Tindle shelled out £1,000 in bets with £650 riding on Farnborough beating Arsenal at 40/1; £250 for the underdogs to score the first goal of the game at 12/1; and £100 on them to win the FA Cup at odds of 10,000/1. If all three bets came off, Sir Ray pledged the £1m to a local hospital appeal. Unfortunately Surrey side Farnborough lost Sir Ray's stake at the first hurdle by losing 1–5 to the Gunners.

Beck's hair changes don't please mum

David Beckham admitted that his mother doesn't always approve of his often-changing hairstyles – and she's a hairdresser. Mickey-taking by opposition fans about his hairstyles is water off a duck's back to Becks, but they also provide humour for his own supporters too. When still with Manchester United he ran out against Deportivo La Coruna with a new longer style, which looked uncannily like a mullet. He was greeted by an unfamiliar chant from the adoring Stretford End: "There's only one Rod Stewart."

Handed a ban

Top international referee Massimo Busacca was suspended for three matches in 2009 for making hand gestures to fans at a Swiss cup game between FC Baden and Young Boys. The incident, captured by a photographer, came after a pitch invasion.

The Bible is unclear on bookings

For devout Christian players such as former Middlesbrough midfield hard man George Boateng there is the question of balancing their faith against illegal acts on the field such as a fouling. Dutchman Boateng once defended his red-and-yellow-card-littered disciplinary record with gusto. How does he reconcile being a devout Christian with his no-nonsense style on the pitch? "I read the Bible but nowhere does it say I must pull out of a tackle," said Boateng. "Just because I'm a Christian it doesn't mean I'm not allowed to get a booking."

Bending it like Beckham

An 11-year-old schoolboy player set a new world record in 2003 for scoring goals direct from corners. Steve Cromley grabbed a first-half hat-trick for Ash Green United in the Coventry Minor League. Each kick sailed in without anyone else touching it with the boy insisting he meant every one. Inspired by the dead-ball excellence of players such as then England captain David Beckham, Steve said he practised for hours swinging the ball. It paid off for Ash Green as Steve's tricky treble helped them to a 10–3 win over Dunlop FC. Steve's impressive feat surpassed that of another schoolboy, Daniel White from Somerset, who several years before scored three by the same method but over 90 minutes instead of in just the first half.

Goal drought

Andrea Silenzi became the first Italian to play in the English Premier League when Nottingham Forest paid £1.8m for his goal-poaching abilities. He failed to score a league goal in two years.

Keeper swaps Spain for rain

Some Spanish sun shone on Lancashire and Cheshire League B Division team Old Chorltonians for a short time in 2003 when an unexpected star landed. Leading Spanish goalkeeper Jonay Cabrera Padron, used to playing in front of 20,000-plus crowds for Las Palmas in the Spanish league, turned up and asked to try out for the amateur side in Manchester. In Britain studying English for only nine months, Padron wanted to stay fit. His experience and skill soon helped Old Chorltonians launch a successful run before his time in rainy Manchester was up. Padron said: "The weather was not great. Several times I had flu."

4 u via txt – you're fired

An Italian football manager found himself out of a job via a text message on his mobile phone. Daniele Carassai, the coach of semi-professional outfit Gotico, was expecting a friendly call from a friend when his phone bleeped. A text message simply said: "You're sacked" and, amazingly, the man doing the sacking, Gotico chairman Andrea Pollastri, thought he was being kind. He said: "I thought it was a far friendlier way of breaking the news." Carassai disagreed saying: "It's not exactly the best way to find out you've lost your job. I was amazed when I read the message and at first thought it was a joke."

High pressure

Frank Worthington failed a medical for a dream move to Liverpool in 1971 because he had high blood pressure blamed on excessive sexual activity. He was told to go on a relaxing holiday and report for a second check-up. He failed that as well because in Majorca he had continued with his womanising high life

Manager's memorabilia up for sale

Colchester United organised an "everything must go" internet sale of monogrammed kit left behind by former boss Steve Whitton. With the club as a player and manager for nine years Whitton left in 2003 without managing them to promotion but in danger of relegation from the English league Second Division. Colchester's online auction took bids for Whitton's training kit, including trousers, shorts, socks and rain jacket – all complete with the "SW" initials.

Penalties down to a fine art

Football was the inspiration of an ever-changing piece of art in 2003. In a unique collaboration Antonio Becerro – Chile's equivalent of Damien Hirst – had top player and compatriot Francisco Huaiquipan take penalties against him using a freshly painted football. The goal was a large white canvas and the work of art changed every time Colo Colo player Huaiquipan struck the ball. Becerro said: "Even the missed penalties produced art because the ball splashed me and the canvas."

Ronaldo, Ronaldo – and Ronaldo

Organisers of the famous 2003 Rio de Janeiro Carnival drafted in a group of 130 Ronaldo lookalikes to open the event. The group, men and women, were dressed in exact replicas of the kit Ronaldo wore during the winning of the 2002 World Cup – right down to the boots and the disastrous two-tone flat-iron haircut modelled by the Brazilian striker during the tournament. Carnival organisers even hired Paulo Cesar Carvalho, the official hairdresser to the Brazilian football team, to ensure hairstyle authenticity. The Rio Carnival is a wild four-day annual celebration before the beginning of Lent.

One-game wonder

Everton manager David Moyes paid £5m for a Denmark international centre half in 2005 but very quickly decided Per Kroldrup wasn't for him. Kroldrup played one game before being sold to Fiorentina.

A pizza the action

Pizza was allegedly thrown at coach Sir Alex Ferguson after a fiery match between his Manchester United and English Premiership arch-rivals Arsenal. The pizza, flavour unknown, was thrown by an Arsenal player during a post-match fracas in the tunnel.

Forlan stud row ends in sale

Diego Forlan revealed how a few millimetres in the length of studs got him booted out of Manchester United. The row with Sir Alex Ferguson over his choice of footwear ended in the Uruguayan being sold to Villarreal in 2004. Ferguson wanted him to play with long studs, which suit wet pitches, but Forlan felt more comfortable in short ones. He defied Ferguson and missed a great chance in a match United lost against Chelsea. Forlan recalls: "I rushed to the dressing room to change boots but Ferguson caught me. He grabbed the boots and threw them. That was my last game for United."

Who wants to be a Millonarios?

A six-month deal with a top Colombian club was the prize in a South American game show. Julian Martinez Cabrera, 17, landed a deal with Club Deportivo Los Millonarios after seeing off 10,000 other hopefuls to win the race for a short contract. Cabrera, who got his big chance when he won the majority of votes from both the judging panel and the audience of the reality TV show, said he was hopeful of ultimately making the Millonarios' first team. A Millonarios spokesman said: "Julian is very good."

Nico-lost

Prolific French striker Nicolas Anelka had to hire a chauffeur when he joined Manchester City in 2002 because he kept getting lost on his way to the club training ground. Then, first time out, the chauffeur got lost too.

Grenade fear for Dalglish

Former Liverpool manager Kenny Dalglish was the innocent victim of a business feud that saw a grenade left at his Birkdale home in 2009. Two men who planned the grenade attack on a Merseyside businessman were jailed for abandoning the device outside the Dalglish home. It was intended to be thrown through a window at Dalglish's neighbour, but the plan was foiled by undercover police before the attack. Two men were jailed for five years and four and a half years respectively.

Wine whine

Chinese officials accused Italian football clubs Inter Milan and Lazio of racking up a £6,000 wine bill during a 2009 trip for a friendly match at Beijing's Bird's Nest Stadium.

Mum's football strip

A young mother got her kit off to give her son a dream trip to the 2003 Worthington Cup final. She posed as a nude model for an art class and won two free tickets to see Manchester United play Liverpool at Cardiff's Millennium Stadium. The young mum spotted a competition in her local paper asking people what they would be prepared to do to get their hands on tickets. She submitted her outrageous suggestion but admitted she hoped she wouldn't win. But she did and said: "I was dreading a phone call and it took a bit of nerve to take my clothes off." She went to the final with United fan son, who saw his side beaten 2–0.

Fatal joke

Lazio midfielder Luciano Re Cecconi's sense of humour was his downfall. In 1978 he walked into a Rome jewellery shop and shouted "Stop! This is a robbery." The shop owner shot Cecconi, who died trying to explain the joke.

Walk-out

Half of Sheffield Wednesday's players in the 1886–87 season defected to another local side because Wednesday were not in the prestigious FA Cup. A club official had forgotten to enter them.

Ref is off

Fans watched in amazement when a referee walked out of an English First Division match in 1914. The official, H. Smith, had sent off Oldham Athletic full back Billy Cook who refused to go. Smith walked off, abandoning the match 30 minutes early.

Two goals in two minutes for keeper

Grays Athletic goalkeeper has the distinction of scoring two goals in two minutes. In a match versus Hendon in 1995, he drop-kicked a ball that bounced in the D of the other penalty area and crept in just under the crossbar. This was in the second minute of first-half stoppage time. In the second minute of the second half and ironically in the same net in which he had scored, he touched an indirect free kick into his own goal.

Len's a uniting spirit

Len Shackleton, one of the most talented inside forwards of the 1940s and 1950s, had a way of uniting city clubs that were usually pitched against each other in intense rivalry. He was a rare beast in being a favourite with both Newcastle United and Sunderland supporters when with their teams. Although a Bradford City fan he was signed to Bradford Park Avenue and once turned out for both clubs on the same day. He had an impish sense of humour and famously, in his autobiography Clown Prince of Soccer, he had a chapter headed: *The Average Director's Knowledge of Football*, which was just an empty page.

Goal blocker

Goalkeeper Willie Foulke was probably the fattest ever to play in English first-class football. The 22 stone 3 lb giant, nicknamed Fatty, who played for Chelsea and won the FA Cup of 1902 with Sheffield United, blew up to 25 stone by the time he joined Bradford City in 1906.

Benin's clean sweep – of sackings

Benin sacked the entire team and coaching staff following their first-round exit from the 2010 Africa Cup of Nations. Ironically, the sweeping change came after the country's joint-highest showing at the tournament. In 2004 and 2008 the squad failed to earn a point but in 2010 they drew with Mozambique, whom they pipped to third in Group C on goal difference. It would seem there was no disgrace in the third spot because the Squirrels were behind eventual winners Egypt and semi-finalists Nigeria. The FA cited a lack of patriotism and mass indiscipline as the reasons for the cull.

Striker offered as shares

Many people will be hoping that young Norwegian striker Daniel Forlandsaas will turn out to be a thoroughbred at his trade because they have horseracing-style shares in him. Pieces of the action were being offered via the internet in 2010 to investors prepared to gamble that Forlandsaas will make the big time. The offer to potential investors, who pay €2,000 annually, is a 10 per cent share in the 20-year-old and a chance to profit from any subsequent transfer fees.

Edmundo hits back at cruelty claims

Brazilian player Edmundo hit back in 1999 over claims that animals were mistreated at a party for his son's first birthday. After facing prosecution by animal welfare groups Edmundo, who had played for 18 clubs in Brazil, Japan and Italy in a 20-year career, proved the accusations were false. The allegations included making a chimpanzee called Pedrinho drunk on beer and whisky.

FIFA strips fans to underpants

Many fans had to watch games at the 2006 World Cup wearing only their underpants because of a ridiculous FIFA demand. Many Dutch fans turned up wearing garish patriotic orange lederhosen carrying the name of a Dutch beer, Bavaria. But because the beer was not an official World Cup sponsor, security staff at Stuttgart made Dutch supporters take their trousers off – leaving many of them to watch Holland's 2–1 victory over the Ivory Coast in their underwear. FIFA was unrepentant, claiming it had done nothing wrong and was entitled to defend itself against what it called "ambush marketing".

Keepy-uppy king

The world keepy-uppy record was smashed by more than four hours in 2009. Dan Magness, 25, kept a football in the air using his feet, legs and head for a marathon 24 hours in front of crowds at London's Covent Garden; the previous record had been 19 hours and 30 minutes. Just seconds away from reaching the 24-hour mark, Magness relaxed as the crowd cheered him on and almost lost control of the ball. He managed to regain his composure and the exhausted Magness passed his magic milestone. The feat went into the *Guinness World Records*, which allowed Magness, from Milton Keynes in southern England, only a few brief pauses in order to relax his muscles.

Spider-Man, Spider-Man!

Ecuador international striker Otilino Tenorio made a name for not only scoring goals, but also celebrating them by pulling on a Spider-Man mask. He died aged 25 in a 2005 car crash.

Naked togetherness

One hundred Rangers and Celtic fans bared all at Scotland's Hampden Park stadium in Glasgow in 2007 as part of the Stripped Naked project to end sectarianism in football.

Rain, rain go away, says Sanchez

Hugo Sanchez blamed his 2009 sacking as manager of Spanish strugglers Almeria on freak rain. Almeria's 4–1 home defeat by Atletico Bilbao came amid heavy rain and Sanchez was sacked after the team's next La Liga defeat, a 2–0 loss at Espanyol. The Mexican goal-scoring legend, who had been in charge at Almeria for a year, said: "It never rains here and the day of the Atletico match it was bucketing down. They put three past us from set pieces and we lost badly." Almeria province is so dry that it was used as the location for numerous spaghetti westerns and the average annual rainfall is just 184 millimetres.

Match fixed

Four players from Liverpool and Manchester United were banned for life in 1915 for their part in a match-fixing scandal. There had been a run of bets on United winning 2–0, which, surprise, surprise, they did.

Unlucky 13

Just 13 people watched a match in Manchester United's vast Old Trafford Stadium on 7 May 1921. They were the hardy fans of Stockport County who had already been relegated and whose ground was under suspension. The 13 had to endure a goalless draw.

Gazza hits the bar

International midfielder Paul Gascoigne went for a drink with pals an hour after playing for England in 1994 – still wearing his full "Three Lions" kit, boots and all.

Three hat-tricks in one game

Three Manchester City players notched hat-tricks in 1987 when the club smashed ten goals past the bottom-of-the-table side Huddersfield Town in an English league Second Division game at Maine Road, Manchester. For a while a goal landslide didn't look likely with Huddersfield dominating the early stages. A Neil McNab goal opened the floodgates before Paul Stewart, Tony Adcock and David White all grabbed three goals each.

Seagulls make pitch unplayable

A football pitch on the Channel Island of Guernsey was rendered unplayable in 2010 – by seagulls. The Blanche Pierre Lane pitch was torn up by aerial vandals and out of action for weeks. The turf at the St Martin's AC's ground had been pulled up by seagulls digging for worms, large areas needed returfing and St Martin's games had to be played elsewhere. Meanwhile, the club protected what little of the field was left untouched with mannequins, normally used for training, acting as scarecrows. The explanation for the bird attack was that the water table was high and the worms near the surface. The seagulls paddled their feet up and down to tease the worms out and damaged the grass at the same time.

Police death

All football in Italy was briefly suspended following the death of a policeman during rioting at a Catania–Palermo match in 2009.

Baptism of fire in first season

Seoul Martyrs lived up to their name in their first season competing in the South Korean third division. Playing in the K3 League turned into a baptism of fire for players and manager and they finished the 2009 season rock bottom. After 32 matches the newly founded club had a goal difference of minus 175, having won just two matches. However, taking the view that from their lowly position the only way is up, the club were taking their place in the division again for the 2010 season.

Schalke fans' premature celebrations

Schalke 04 fans got carried away and started celebrating what they thought was the winning of the Bundesliga title on the final day of the 2000–01 season. Schalke needed to win at home to Unterhaching and hope Hamburg's HSV could beat Bayern Munich. Hearts were in mouths when Schalke went 2–0 down only to pull back to 2–2 before half-time, while over in Hamburg it was 0–0. Schalke then fell 3–2 behind, but celebrations really started with a comeback to win 5–3 and the news that HSV were 1–0 up in the 90th minute. Schalke fans were suddenly silenced when in the 94th minute Bayern squeezed home an equaliser to shave the title.

Starting over

Serie A club Fiorentina was declared bankrupt in 2004 and the new Florence-based club that emerged from the financial wreckage had to start again in Italy's fourth division.

Civic pride

German international striker Miroslav Klose came partly into civic ownership when his Bundesliga team Kaiserslautern sold a share of him to the local council. The move bought the club some vital breathing space during a 2003 financial crisis.

Comeback costs gambler his house

As far as comebacks are concerned it was one of the greatest in the English Premiership. In 2001 Tottenham Hotspur were running rings around Manchester United and 3–0 up at half-time. Betting exchanges were the new thing and a Spurs fan who wanted to impress his girlfriend confidently put his mortgage on a Spurs' win in a short-odds wager – then sat back to make a fortune. The party poopers were never-say-die United who powered back into the game to win 5–3.

Premature pitch invasion

Scarborough fans were ecstatic in 1999. Thousands of them were prancing around on the pitch in celebration of staying in the English league's Third Division. They had gone into the last game of the season knowing they would survive providing their result equalled or bettered that of equally relegation-threatened Carlisle's. Scarborough drew 1–1 with Peterborough and, according to those with radios, Carlisle were also heading for a 1–1 stalemate against Plymouth. Cue a joyful pitch invasion at Scarborough at the final whistle only for it to be silenced by Carlisle's goalkeeper, Jimmy Glass, scoring in the third minute of injury time to send Scarborough down.

Pre-match snifters

Nottingham Forest celebrated winning the 1979 League Cup – the night before they won it. Manager Brian Clough locked his players in a hotel room with a crate of champagne and 10 pints of beer. They beat Southampton 3–2 next day.

Fan's Andy Cole tattoo folly

A fanatical Newcastle United supporter was definitely not showing off his latest tattoo to his mates in 1995. He had chosen to have a large image of prolific striker Andy Cole in full Magpies garb tattooed on to his right thigh – but two days later Cole left for Manchester United. Cole had become a cult hero in his two years at St James' Park and had won the fans' hearts with a scoring record to match greats such as Jackie Milburn. Cole, in just 70 appearances, had hammered 55 goals – a record worth immortalising but perhaps not as permanently as with a tattoo.

Caught by friendly fire

Millwall supporters were so intent on trouble when visiting Bristol City for an English league Second Division match in 2001, they didn't check who they were attacking. According to a report by the National Criminal Intelligence Service (NCIS), as a large group of Millwall supporters were taken under escort towards Ashton Gate Stadium, they passed a public house. From it rushed a group of 30 to 40 men and during the ensuing violent fracas bottles and glasses were thrown, pub windows smashed and a few injuries sustained. After a while it petered out as, rather sheepishly for the protagonists, it became apparent that both groups were from Millwall.

Headline Balls-up

When Everton legend Alan Ball and his father towed a fan's broken-down car from Liverpool's Mersey Tunnel, the local paper related the story with the headline: "Boy pulled out of Mersey Tunnel by the Balls".

Thieves raid dressing room

Thieves who raided an English football club's dressing room rubbed salt in the wound. They stole the keys to one of the player's cars, loaded the vehicle up with their booty of stolen goods before driving off in it. Cash, phones and jewellery were taken after burglars smashed their way into the changing room during the Leicestershire match between Queniborough and Broughton Astley. When the stolen Mini roared off, its owner was alerted and the referee stopped play – with Queniborough winning 6–0 – and the players rushed to the changing room to find the door kicked down.

Fit to faint

Frank Swift, a 19-year-old goalkeeper, was so overcome by winning the 1934 FA Cup final that he fainted at the final whistle. Having played only half a season for Manchester City the moment was too much and he had to be revived to receive his winner's medal.

Repeat performance

Charlie Tully's goal direct from a corner for Celtic against Falkirk in a 1953 Scottish league match was ruled out because the crowd had spilled on to the pitch. He retook it – and scored direct again.

Robinho fights for his right to party

Brazilian striker Robinho's celebrations at featuring in a 5–0 win for his country annoyed his club Real Madrid in 2005. He arrived back late in the Spanish capital after partying with his Brazilian team-mates. There was an even greater excuse for a party because Brazil had hammered Ecuador and Robinho, who wasn't to last much longer at Real, defended the Brazilian right to celebrate their wins. He defiantly declared: "I'm not apologising for the party. Parties are normal with Brazil after we've won a match – and that night we had won 5–0."

"Prankster" fools trouserless star

Arsenal striker Nicklas Bendtner found himself dropped – by his trousers – after a Champions League semi-final defeat by Manchester United in 2009. The young Danish striker was pictured in the media stumbling out of a London nightclub at four in the morning with his trousers round his knees. Both Bendtner and his Arsenal manager Arsene Wenger denied the Dane was drunk and passed off the half-mast trousers as the work of a mystery prankster.

Changing-room raiders strike

Players with Snainton FC in English non-league football had cash and phones stolen from the changing rooms at Bishopthorpe in Yorkshire. The thieves' haul came to thousands of pounds in valuables including £300 in cash and if the Snainton team thought its day could not get worse, they were wrong – they lost their 2009 match to home club Bishopthorpe United 7–0.

Cup replay makes history

For the first time in 127 years and over 50,000 FA Cup ties in England, the Football Association sanctioned a replay even though one of the sides had won the previous encounter. In 1999 Arsenal beat Sheffield United 2–1 in a fifth-round tie with a highly contentious winner. At 1–1 United keeper Alan Kelly had put the ball out of play to allow an injured team-mate to be treated. At the resumption and in the interests of fair play and sporting practice Arsenal's Ray Parlour threw the ball to Kelly, but Kanu intercepted and passed for Overmars to score. There were massed protests by United and Arsenal readily agreed to a replay, which Arsenal also won 2–1.

Bum deal

Shooting at the Club America club in Mexico City had a different meaning in 2010 when two players were the victims of a gun attack. Striker Salvador Cabañas amazingly survived a shot to the head which left him in intensive care. The Paraguayan was a victim of gunfire in a Mexico City bar. A week later, his Mexican teammate, Juan Carlos Silva, became the second Club America star to be shot. This time the gunman's aim was lower and the bullet passed through Silva's buttock.

Salute scandal

Diplomats forced England's players into a humiliating Nazi salute before their 1938 international in Berlin against Germany. The British ambassador did not want to snub Hitler's Germany, but the English players got revenge with a 6–3 win. Only Stan Cullis refused and was disciplined.

Mole hits fixtures' schedule

An itinerant mole caused Lincoln United to cancel a match in 2009 because it had left molehills all over the pitch. The club called off a game with Lincoln City reserves after the ground became littered with more molehills than the grounds staff could cope with. Wildlife experts reckoned the mole was probably a juvenile trying to find its own territory, although they admitted it is unlikely that the animal would escape the traps that were scattered across the pitch.

Vinnie's all heart

Hardman Vinnie Jones put in a few heart-stopping tackles during his 13-year professional football career but in 2012 he was credited with saving the lives of heart attack victims. The midfielder, who became an actor after playing for Wimbledon, Chelsea, Leeds and Sheffield United, was the star of a "Staying Alive" ad campaign focusing on what to do if someone has a heart attack. In 15 cases that happened soon after the ad was aired, lives were saved because helpers followed Vinnie's advice on pushing down on the chest in time to the Bee Gees' hit "Stayin' Alive".

Own goal

One of the greatest moments in a footballer's life is lifting the World Cup as the winning captain. But this ultimate football honour was denied Brazil's Emerson in 2002 because the midfielder opted to play in goal in a training match. He dislocated his shoulder trying to save a Rivaldo shot and Cafu replaced him as the victorious captain at the tournament held in South Korea and Japan.

Ronaldo lookalike scores too

Looking like Real Madrid's star Cristiano Ronaldo has benefits for Jaime Wright from Eastbourne in England. In 2010 he made his living as a professional lookalike, turning up at parties to stand around resembling the Portuguese winger. He revealed he used his Ronaldo resemblance to get unsuspecting women to sleep with him. He was reported as saying: "I was in a club in Manchester and these three girls just came up and said, 'You are Ronaldo.' I didn't say that I was; and I didn't say I wasn't. We went back to a hotel and had a great night. I tell them they are very beautiful in Portuguese and I sometimes put the accent on as well. Some girls haven't realised I am not the real deal until the next morning."

TV for me

Argentina coach Diego Maradona announced in 2010 that he was launching a TV channel in his native country to feature his and the lives of other sports stars.

Hot stuff

Kevin Kyle was christened "Scaldin' Balls" in 2006 after injuring his private parts with a jug of boiling water. The proud dad was warming up a bottle of milk for his new son when the toddler slipped and hit the jug in Kyle's direction, inflicting burns to his testicles and inner thigh. The Scot was forced to miss Sunderland's next game because he "walked like John Wayne" according to a member of the coaching staff.

Pegasus fly

A team with no ground who did not play in a league won England's Amateur Cup in 1951. Pegasus was a scratch team of Oxford and Cambridge university graduates who played away games only. They beat Bishop Auckland, who were in their 14th final, 2–1.

Strip cartoon beats photo ban

A dispute between Hartlepool United and two of its local newspapers ended with some of the media being barred from reporting games. The Hartlepool Mail was red-carded in 2008 by the club for refusing to sign a commercial agreement, then the Northern Echo was barred for supplying the Mail with match photographs. While the dispute ground on the Echo reported from the terraces instead of the press box and got around the photography ban by producing a Roy of the Rovers-style strip cartoon of the day's action.

Paying lip service to team bonding

Love it or loathe it, footballers kissing has been a part of the modern game since the 1960s. But the quick congratulatory peck on the cheek is not enough for Miroslav Ciro Blazevic. In 2009 the national team coach for Bosnia-Herzegovina ordered his players to kiss full on the lips as part of a team-bonding exercise. He said kissing on the lips fostered team unity: "I take two of my players and tell them 'love him, kiss him.'" He added: "The secret of my success is in a unity of a squad. You can't do anything without an atmosphere in a team."

Numbers first

Numbers were worn for the first time in the 1933 English FA Cup final. Everton, eventual 3–0 winners, were numbered from 1 to 11, while opponents Manchester City were from 12 to 22 with the goalkeeper as the latter.

Ticket gamble over baby's birth

Football-mad Vince Reeves risked missing the birth of his first child in order to get FA Cup tickets. The Southampton fan and wife Rebecca had been queuing for tickets for 90 minutes when she went into labour. Not wanting to lose his place in the queue Vince arranged for a friend to take his wife home and when her waters broke Vince was still 50 places from the front of the queue, so his mother-in-law took Rebecca to hospital. Vince still managed to get the tickets for a 2010 tie against Portsmouth and be at his wife's side in time for the birth of daughter Jessica, who has been given a lifelong season ticket by the club. The only downside was Vince watched Southampton lose 4–1.

Paying for fun

Dundee United manager from 1971 to 1993, Jim McLean, withheld a win bonus from his entire squad for failing to provide "enough entertainment" – United had beaten Motherwell 6–1.

Beckhams give £1m to charity

David and Victoria Beckham gave £1m to a children's charity over five years from 2005 to 2010. The money has bought, among other things, state-of-the-art wheelchairs to improve the lives of many disabled children. Some wheelchairs cost up to £10,000. The Victoria and David Beckham Children's Charity was run by Posh's mother Jackie.

Own-goal strategy is a winner

The sight of two sides defending furiously did not make for an attacking game when Barbados met Grenada in a 1994 Shell Caribbean Cup match. Barbados just needed a two-goal winning margin to progress instead of Grenada and the equation was further complicated by the decision that a golden goal in extra time would count double. At 2–1 to Barbados, the Bajans saw that was not enough so a deliberate own goal by a defender made it 2–2 – and extra time. Barbados won with the golden goal.

Payne for Rovers

Reserve wing half Joe Payne was called up by Luton Town as an emergency centre forward for an English Third Division match in 1936 – and proceeded to score a record ten goals in a 12-0 win over Bristol Rovers.

Bare body campaign fails

German Green Party MPs Evelin Schonhut-Keil and Margareta Wolf launched a campaign to end the rule of giving yellow cards to players whipping their shirts off in celebration. Inspired by Cristiano Ronaldo's buff torso on show at Euro 2004 they wrote to the German FA without success. They took their campaign to FIFA, whose president Sepp Blatter had called for skimpier clothing for female footballers, again to no avail. In their letter to the German FA they said: "We can't understand how the voluntary showing of a gorgeous male chest can be objectionable."

Won by a neck

Former German prisoner of war Bert Trautmann unknowingly played for the last 15 minutes of the 1956 English FA Cup final with a broken neck. His reward was a 3–1 win for Manchester City over Birmingham City.

Ref red-cards 14 ball boys

Every ball boy at a match in Spain was sent off by a frustrated referee in 2006. Real Betis were 1–0 up at home to Atletico Madrid when the ball boys went on strike. Allegedly following orders from club officials, the boys refused to put the ball back into play as six minutes of added time ticked away. Atletico were furious and the referee Miguel Ayza Gamez sent off all 14 ball boys. Chelsea once had a similar complaint against Real Betis because the ball boys disappeared once Chelsea had fallen behind.

All for one

Shirt manufacturer Puma's all-in-one shirt and shorts design for teams at the 2004 Africa Cup of Nations was banned by FIFA.

Gazza's impulses

England midfielder Paul Gascoigne was prone to acting on impulse off the field. He astounded London commuters by jumping on a double-decker bus in Piccadilly Circus and asking if he could take control. Amazingly, the bus driver agreed and passengers got an impromptu show of Gazza's driving skills. On another occasion in the capital, Gascoigne jumped out of his car and asked a workman if he could have "a go" on a pneumatic drill. He then set about pounding the pavement to the amusement of onlookers.

Sleeve us alone

Sleeveless shirts planned for the 2002 World Cup finals for Cameroon were banned by FIFA for being "in breach of regulations". The team still wore them, but with black t-shirts underneath.

Pope was a supporter of football

No pope has been more synonymous with football than Pope John Paul II. He played in goal in his native Poland and even as Pontiff he took a keen interest in the world game. Several clubs were said to have been named as his favourites, such as Cracovia Krakow, Liverpool and Barcelona. London club Fulham were also mentioned in connection with the Pope, but that turned out to be a myth promoted by the media. Pope John Paul couldn't have, as reported, stood on the Craven Cottage terraces as a young priest in 1930 because he would have been only ten at the time and was not ordained until 1946. A British newspaper that doctored a picture of the Pope to show him wearing a Fulham scarf was forced to apologise.

Life's a Bitchy

Canada's Toronto FC brought in a Harris hawk called Bitchy in 2007 to help keep their stadium clear of seagulls attracted from nearby Lake Ontario to enjoy a good meal on the litter left after matches.

Fans threaten hunger strike

Long-distance sponsors withdrew their support for FC Moscow in 2010 and forced the club into a financial crisis. Norilsk, the world's biggest nickel and palladium producer, said it would no longer finance the team because it is too far from the company's base in the Siberian city of Norilsk, 3,000 kilometres away from the capital Moscow. Fans threatened to go on hunger strike to protest against the club's pulling out of the Russian Premier League and were trying to get government help. FC Moscow was formed after the demise of Torpedo Moscow in 2004, and regularly attracted the lowest attendance in the Premier League.

Serial collector

Former butcher Anton Johnson was banned from football for life by the English FA in 1985 because he had broken the rules by having interests in Southend, Bournemouth and Rotherham at the same time. He had also approached Scarborough and Doncaster Rovers.

Heatwave hits football

Referees were ordered to take pitch temperatures before allowing matches to go ahead in southern Brazil in the midsummer of 2010. The heatwave caused postponements and led a judge in the state of Rio Grande do Sul to ban matches when the temperature exceeded 35°C. Judge Rafael da Silva Marques banned day-time matches after several players felt ill during a match in the state's Gaucho Championship that kicked off in 40°C heat, then ruled that evening games could only go ahead after the referee had checked the temperature on the pitch.

Friendly abandoned after ref attack

A referee attacked, opposition coach assaulted and a pitch invasion by incensed club officials was the outcome of a game staged in Turkey – and it was a friendly. Staged between Bulgaria's Slavia Sofia and Russian club Anzhi Makhachkala in the Turkish resort of Antalya, the 2010 game was abandoned. Trouble started when Anzhi officials, led by their club president, rushed on to the pitch after substitute Magomed Magomedov, incidentally the president's son, was sent off for a second bookable offence. TV footage showed the Ukrainian referee and Slavia coach Velislav Vutsov appearing to be pushed and struck after being surrounded by a dozen Anzhi officials and players.

First lady

It took 43 years for the BBC to appoint a woman to commentate on a match for its flagship Saturday-night football programme Match of the Day. The ground-breaking lady was Jacqui Oatley.

Player PoW

Prolific England scorer Steve Bloomer was interned for the whole of World War 1. He had been coaching in Germany and was arrested at the outbreak of hostilities.

Hit for six

Arthur Rowley signed for Leicester City from Fulham, then in the 1952–53 season he scored hat-tricks against his old club both times he met them.

Charity stunt goes wrong

If he thought 2002 was a bad year for injuries, jinxed Coventry midfielder Keith O'Neill reckoned without a fairground test-your-strength machine. The Republic of Ireland international was out of action but decided to use his spare time nobly in supporting a charity event. There he took a mighty swing at the punchbag and broke his hand. That injury was his third in a few months, having broken his leg at the end of previous season and then fractured a foot.

Striking duo hammer each other

Eyewitnesses said Hull City team-mates Marlon King and Dean Windass brawled "like snarling animals" in a casino fight in 2008. It was alleged King headbutted Windass before the pair were pulled apart. King is then said to have fired insults at staff and allegedly tried to cause more trouble at the Scarborough Casino in Yorkshire by pretending his £19,000 watch had been stolen, but it was found in his pocket. It was said there had been tension between the two since King replaced veteran Windass as Hull's main striker.

Just kidding?

Dutchman Rafael van der Vaart was dubbed "van der Farce" by the German media in 2007 for claiming he had been injured – by his one-year-old son. The Hamburg midfielder pulled out of a European game claiming that lifting the boy had injured his back. What enraged the press – and Hamburg fans – was that it was well-known that the player was desperate to leave for Valencia in Spain so he didn't want to be cup-tied at Hamburg.

Peru riot

One of the biggest losses of life in a football disaster was the result of Peruvian fans rioting at the national stadium in Lima after their team's goal against Argentina was disallowed. Three hundred people died.

Players zapped

TV remote controls have been responsible for a number of Premier League players missing games after suffering injuries stretching for the "zapper". Tottenham striker Robbie Keane and Chelsea goalkeeper Carlo Cudicini suffered knee injuries while Portsmouth keeper David James pulled a muscle in his back. Arsenal's David Seaman also pulled a muscle as he tried to record Coronation Street.

Pool fool

An international goalkeeper was dropped from his country's 1982 World Cup team after pretending to have drowned in the swimming pool at the team's hotel.

Lost boots

The boots of the whole Colombian national squad disappeared while on a European tour in 2006. They were lost en route to Germany from Poland where they had helped Colombia to a 2–1 win over the hosts.

Gay team remembers Fashanu

A football team in England named itself after a gay striker who committed suicide. The Justin Fashanu All-stars were launched in 2008 supported by the English FA in memory of the former Nottingham Forest and Norwich player who was 37 when he was found hanged in 1998. The new team was created by the Justin Campaign, which promotes the inclusion of openly gay players in football. The pink and black team kit was sponsored by DJ Norman Cook, better known as Fatboy Slim, and the side was open to gay and straight footballers. Justin was the UK's first professional footballer to be open about his homosexuality. In the early 1980s he was rated as one of English football's brightest young stars, but his career took a nosedive after a £1m move to Nottingham Forest and a serious knee injury.

Manager sells himself – as a player

Player-manager Ivan Broadis sold himself to another club in 1949 to boost the finances of the team he was leaving. Broadis became at 23 the youngest player-manager ever when he went to Carlisle United in 1946. But with the club's finances ever tenuous, he saw a chance to leave a financial legacy for Carlisle and sold himself to Sunderland for £18,000. After a career that won 18 England caps and took him to Manchester City, he returned to Carlisle as a journalist on the local paper.

Successive successes

Cliff Holton became the first English league player to score hat-tricks on successive days. He scored for Watford in a 4–2 win over Chester and again in a 5–0 victory over Gateshead during the 1960 Easter programme.

Players make a long-player

Many squads have recorded songs but few clubs have attempted to crash the album market. Tottenham Hotspur players cut an LP in 1967 to be released with their hit cup final single "Glory Glory Hallelujah". It contained such tracks as "Bye, Bye Blackbird" by Terry Venables; Jimmy Greaves singing "Strollin'"; Scottish squad members extolling "I Belong to Glasgow"; and its Irishmen such as Pat Jennings and Joe Kinnear with "When Irish Eyes Are Smiling". It made a small impact on the album chart of the time but unfortunately it was released at the same time as a rather more iconic album, The Beatles' Sgt Pepper's Lonely Hearts Club Band.

Eye, eye

Six Newcastle United players, including goalkeeper Shay Given, were ruled out of the start of the 2004–05 season after an outbreak of the contagious eye disease conjunctivitis.

Arsenal's blue reminder of rivals

Given the modern-day bitterness between the two north London sides – Tottenham Hotspur and Arsenal – the clubs are closer than many of their respective fans would believe. In fact, the Arsenal badge carries a blue border in thanks to Spurs. During World War 2 Arsenal's Highbury ground was commandeered by the government and the Gunners were given shared use of Tottenham's White Hart Lane. As a thank you, legend has it, the Arsenal board promised always to have a little Tottenham blue in their mainly red and white strip, even if it is only on the badge.

Myhre is mired

Just as Norwegian goalkeeper Thomas Myhre returned to full fitness with club side Everton after breaking his ankle while on duty with Norway's national side, he fell in the bath – breaking his other ankle.

Shouldering the blame

Fenerbahce's Volkan Demirel dislocated his shoulder when he fell over while throwing his shirt to fans after a 2004 2–1 win against Turkish league rivals Galatasaray. He was out for three weeks.

Hic, hic hooray

Brazilian league referee José Roberto Marques denied being drunk in charge of a match in 2012 despite continually laughing at the players and getting a ball boy to take a corner. However, the ref, who was spotted drinking 20 cups of water before kick-off, was suspended after CCTV footage showed him hours before the game buying alcohol at a service station while being held upright by a number of girls. Marques claimed his bizarre antics during the match were down to "anxiety".

First sponsor

In 1976 Kettering Town became the first British team to have shirt sponsorship. Kettering Tyres were the sponsors, but Town chief executive Derek Dougan was ordered by the FA to remove the slogan. He changed it to "Kettering T" claiming the "T" stood for Town.

Mowed down

Slicing off one of his toes in a freak lawn-mowing accident meant Wycombe Wanderers goalkeeper Frank Talia missed the start of the 2004–05 season.

Team walks off – after two minutes

A game between two bitter Egyptian rivals lasted just two minutes. That is all it took for the game to degenerate to farcical levels. The scene for confrontation was set because the 1999 Cairo derby between Al-Ahly and Zamalek had to be staged in a neutral stadium for security reasons. Even a neutral French referee was drafted in and he started the walk-off fiasco by dismissing a Zamalek player for an early tackle from behind. His team-mates stormed off in protest and refused to continue. Zamalek was fined by the Egyptian FA for its players' actions.

Player is paid £2.05m per game

Making four starts for Chelsea in four years between 2000 and 2004, earning around £8.2m in the process, did not faze Winston Bogarde. He shamelessly admitted he didn't consider leaving Stamford Bridge despite the promptings of a club keen to cut its wage bill. In his autobiography *This Black Man Bows for No One* he defiantly explained his thinking that his contract was wholeheartedly signed on both sides and he saw no reason to break his side of it. He said: "This world is about money so when you are offered millions, you take them. I may have been one of the worst buys in Premiership history but I don't care."

Playing upfront?

Previous to her successful career as a busty model, singer and actress Samantha Fox played as a 14-year-old for Arsenal Ladies.

Brotherly force

Brothers Leslie and Denis Compton stole the show when Arsenal beat Clapton Orient 15–2 in a 1941 match. Leslie, normally a full back, scored ten and Denis weighed in with two.

Number ones clash

Gillingham's Vince Bartram broke his wrist in a league game against Millwall in 2003 when he collided with opposite number Tony Warner, who had come up for a last-minute corner.

Player gets antsy

Marcos Paulo stunned the watching Brazilian crowd and the referee by suddenly sprinting off the field to the dressing room in the middle of a Santacruzense match in 2008. The player had been rolling on the pitch in order to gain a foul but had inadvertently disturbed an ants' nest. Within seconds his chest, sides and legs were a swarming black mass. The ref, who didn't understand the player's predicament, tried to book Paulo before he rolled in a puddle, then sprinted to the showers to wash away the frenzied biting insects. He said afterwards: "They hurt like hell."

Million misses

Battling team-mates wrecked Bristol Rovers' goalkeeper Esmond Million's chance of a £300 reward for throwing a game in 1963. The team, unaware of Million's corruption, drew 2–2. Million was fined £50 under the Prevention of Corruption Act and banned from football for life.

Church welcomes world champion

In a cruel twist of fate a goalkeeper with a World Cup medal played for a lowly church team in Italy between the 1994 and 1998 World Cups. Brazil's Taffarel found himself without a professional team because his Italian employers Reggiana had a full quota of foreign players and couldn't utilise the man who had won the 1994 World Cup. Unemployed for seven months, he played for the Church of the Most Precious Blood team – as a striker. After seven games in which he scored 15 goals, Taffarel managed to get a club in Brazil and was back in contention for his national team by the 1998 World Cup finals.

Numbers game

Barry Town goalkeeper Lee Kendall had a jersey with no number for a UEFA Cup preliminary tie in 2000 and the ref ordered him to get one. Barry officials fashioned Lee's squad number, 25, out of masking tape before Kendall could carry on. Moments later the tape came off and blew away.

Unlucky strike

Danish footballer Jonathan Richter was left in a coma after being struck by lightning during a 2009 match in Copenhagen. He recovered but lost part of a leg.

Two-touch penalties not such a rarity

Rarely employed but almost always successful, two-touch penalties inside the box are legal. Famous duos such as Jesper Olsen/Johan Cruyff of Ajax and Thierry Henry/Robert Pires of Arsenal are the most famous exponents but its use goes back to 1957 when a three-touch version was used in an Iceland–Belgium international. Already 6–1 up before half-time Belgium were awarded a penalty that Rik Coppens touched to Andre Piters who returned it for Coppens to score. It was also a successful ploy regularly used by England's Plymouth Argyle in the 1960s.

Mystery of the missing cup winners

"The Public" is probably what should be inserted in the list of winners of the Scottish FA Cup for 1909. History has left it blank because there was no winner – on the pitch at least. With the ever-dominant Glasgow clubs Celtic and Rangers drawing the first final 2–2, word spread like wildfire among disgruntled fans that the Scottish Football Association was fixing draws to make extra money from the replays. So when the second game at Hampden Park was a 1–1 draw with no extra time, the paranoia was confirmed in the eyes of the fans. In a bizarre united front, given their normal sectarian divide, spectators from both sides rioted for two hours. The tie was abandoned with no winner declared and no medals given to players.

Stress protection

Paul Hucker insured himself for £1m against the trauma of seeing England knocked out of the early stages of the 2006 World Cup. He paid £105 for the World Cup All Risks policy and said: "A lot of supporters are under a lot of pressure." England reached the quarter-finals.

Streaker is a striker, too

Serial streaker Mark Roberts actually "scored" goals on two big-match occasions when he got his kit off and dashed into a game. In a 2000 match between Chelsea and Liverpool at Anfield an absolutely naked Roberts intercepted a pass, dribbled through the astounded Chelsea defence and "scored". The streaking Briton repeated this in the 2002 Champions League final when he found the Bayer Leverkusen net in their game against Real Madrid. As this was at Hampden Park, Glasgow, Roberts wore only a Tam O'Shanter for the occasion.

London calling for cup duty

European football rules for the first Inter-City Fairs Cup meant that a mixed team from London clubs reached the 1958 final. The rules of the time stipulated that only one team per city was allowed so a very strong London XI was put together from players from all over the metropolis. There were representatives of the top clubs Arsenal, Tottenham Hotspur, Chelsea and West Ham, but even players from lowly Brentford and Leyton Orient were selected. In the final, London drew 2–2 with Barcelona at home but were slaughtered 6–0 in the Spanish leg.

Moose crash

Norwegian defender Svein Grondalen missed an international match in 1974 because he was injured colliding with a moose while on a training run.

Witch doctors a double-edged sword

Australia learned the hard way about double-crossing witch doctors. In a bizarre piece of history, the Australian national side employed a witch doctor in 1969 in a bid to help them beat Rhodesia (now Zimbabwe) and enhance their chances of making the 1970 World Cup finals. But after winning 3–1 the ungrateful Aussies refused to pay the £1,000 demanded and promptly had the "curse" turned on them. Apart from qualifying for the 1974 World Cup finals, Australia's form went into decline until a different witch doctor reversed the "curse", again enabling Australia to qualify for the 2006 finals.

Battle hots up to get frozen games on

The winter of 1962–63 was a severe one by Britain's standards and players were idle for months as the "Big Freeze" held from December to March with some pitches frozen to a depth of four inches. Clubs tried some revolutionary ways to get games on. Norwich City drafted in flamethrowers to try to thaw their Carrow Road ground but as soon as the ice on the surface melted it froze again. Blackpool used a farm harrow to no avail and Dundee United used a lorry-based road tar burner to thaw out the Tannadice pitch but it totally destroyed the grass. The match went ahead after lorry-loads of sand were dumped on the pitch.

Spate of eight

Jim Dyet scored an incredible eight goals on his first-class football debut. His King's Park team hammered Forfar 12–2 in a Scottish Second Division game in 1930.

Hitting the right notes – off the field

Many players have had a double life, flirting with a music career, however fleeting. Former Tottenham and England midfielders Glenn Hoddle and Chris Waddle recorded "Diamond Lights" in 1987 and reached No. 12 in the pop charts. Hamburg's Kevin Keegan's "Head Over Heels In Love" reached No. 33 in 1979, and Chelsea stars Didier Drogba and Michael Essien lent their vocals to anti-racism song "Skins" in 2007. When playing in Germany, Paraguayan striker Roque Santa Cruz made the Top 40 there and in Austria. Carlos Tevez was the front man of an Argentinian band called Piola Vago and Blackburn's Morten Gamst Pedersen fronted a Norwegian boy band of footballers called, appropriately enough, The Players.

Sweet 16 is a record

Two players have performed the Herculean feat of scoring a record 16 goals in a match. In 1942 in wartime France Stephan Stanis blasted 16 for Racing Club in a French Cup massacre of minnows Aubry Asturies. It was 65 years before a similar feat was achieved when in Cyprus Panagiotis Pontikos of Olympos Xylofagou destroyed SEK Ayios Athanasios in 2007. The final score was 24–3 with Pontikos entering the *Guinness Book of Records*.

Quite a party

Manchester United players, including apprentices, stumped up £4,000 a head to have a reputed £200,000 for the pot for their 2007 Christmas party.

Three in a row for Best and Williams

As George Best came through the ranks as a super-talented 17-year-old his progress became inextricably linked with West Bromwich Albion's full back Graham Williams. When Best made his debut in Manchester United's reserves in 1962 he was marked by the physical presence of Williams, then when Best played his first game for United's first XI, Williams was there again in the West Brom team. Best was soon having his first international for Northern Ireland against Wales. And who should be there in the Welsh team to mark him? – Graham Williams.

Ineligible players spark landslide win

FIFA had a big hand in one of the most fantastic scorelines in World Cup football – the 31–0 destruction of American Samoa by Australia in 2001. In a qualifying group for the 2002 World Cup finals in Japan and South Korea, FIFA declared 19 of the American Samoa squad ineligible because of passport problems. American Samoa were also unable to call in players from their under-20 squad because most of them were involved in high school exams. Coach Tunoa Lui was forced to draft in youth players, including three 15-year-olds, to put together a makeshift team with an average age of 18. Even a weakened Australian side couldn't fail to notch up a record score.

Own goal superstar

A haul of five goals in a match should be cause for celebration – unless you were Doug Hurrell. In a 1982 Essex local league match Hurrell sensationally scored five OWN goals as a defender for Rainsford Eagles. His three deflections and two failed headers off the line contributed to Eagles' thumping 3-13 defeat to Heybridge Social.

Short-term jobs

Scottish-born Tommy Docherty managed three English clubs in just six weeks in 1968. He quit Rotherham on 6 November to become Queen's Park Rangers' boss, then walked out after a row a month later into a job at Aston Villa on 18 December.

Celtic's long wait for trophy

Glasgow Celtic recorded possibly the longest wait ever for a trophy. The club went almost three-quarters of a century, including two World Wars, between the match and finally getting their hands on the cup they won. Celtic were triumphant on a pre-World War 1 tour of Europe and beat English side Burnley in Budapest to claim the Ferencvaros Vase to mark their triumph of 1914. The war intervened and the years went by without receiving the trophy from Hungary. A second World War went by and still no trophy, until 74 years later it was presented in Celtic's centenary year of 1987. Only then was it revealed that the original metal vase had been melted down in the war effort of 1914 and the 1987 version finally nestling in the Celtic Park trophy room was porcelain.

Socrates returns

Socrates, the Brazilian captain of two World Cups in the 1980s, returned a decade after retiring to turn out for English Northern Counties team Garforth Town – for 20 minutes.

Welcoming fire

Wimbledon's "Crazy Gang" squad was known for its pranks. They welcomed £7.5m signing John Hartson in 1999 by burning his new Armani suit.

Ref's celebration earns reprimand

A referee's neutrality was called into question in 2000 when he pumped his fist in the air and shouted "Yes!" as one of the teams scored. At the time it looked like a touch of partisanship towards Liverpool, who had just scored through Patrik Berger in the English Premier League against Leeds United. Called upon to explain his actions, ref Mike Reed claimed he was celebrating his own inspiration as he had allowed the game to flow after a foul had been committed but Liverpool still had the advantage. He waved play on and Liverpool made the most of it without the game being stopped. Reed was reprimanded and told to keep his emotions in check in future.

Roberto's as strong as an ox

The power behind the running and shooting of Brazilian full back Roberto Carlos during the 1990s and Noughties was attributed to him being treated as a human ox when growing up. The free-kick specialist with the explosive running speed and powerful curling banana shot grew up in a poor agricultural area near Sao Paulo and was required to work in the fields alongside his father. He developed his impressive thigh power by pushing and pulling agricultural machinery around fields.

Not Keane

The first Sunderland chairman Niall Quinn knew that his manager Roy Keane was resigning in 2008 was a text message on his mobile phone.

Harrod's ban for millionaires

The company owned by Fulham chairman Mohamed Al Fayed dished out a severe snub to Europa League opponents Shakhtar Donetsk before a match in 2010. The millionaire players from the Ukrainian side were thrown out of the famous Harrods store in London for "health and safety reasons". Despite having huge sums to spend the Shakhtar group, which was going shopping after a training session, was deemed too big for the store – but dress code may have been a factor as some were wearing tracksuits. Shakhtar Donetsk also went home empty-handed from the pitch as Fulham won the first leg of the last-32 tie 2–1.

Six red cards in one match

Six red cards in a single match in 2009 effectively ended Paul Cooper's time as a player. Cooper, 39, was sent off for dissent while playing for Hawick United against Pencaitland in the Border Amateur League. But Cooper wouldn't let it go and he then received another five red cards for verbal exchanges with the referee and received a two-year ban and a £150 fine. Mr Cooper said ruefully: "I'll have to find something else to do on a Saturday. I completely overreacted after I had been sent off and I know I said things to the referee I should not have." Cooper had received bans before.

MP's perks

Hungarian captain Jozsef Bozsik escaped punishment for his part in the so-called "Battle of Berne" at the 1954 World Cup finals – because he was a Member of the Hungarian Parliament.

Bent gags himself to end poor run

Former England striker Darren Bent publicly shut down his Twitter site in a bid to end his club's poor run of form in 2010. The Sunderland striker was one of the high-profile "tweets" in Britain with his outspoken use of the social networking site. But with Sunderland tumbling down the English Premier League after a string of poor results he became a Twitter quitter. He said that after discussions with his team manager it was agreed the Sunderland top scorer should spend less time online and more on form in front of goal.

Being Ruud

Ruud Gullit chased a Football Association press officer and the FA Cup out of Newcastle's training ground. The FA man had been on a promotional tour with the trophy but Dutchman Gullit reckoned seeing it before winning it was bad luck. Newcastle still didn't win it in 1999.

Garrincha – bow-legged legend

Double World Cup-winner Garrincha had one of the most colourful lives in the history of football – including the widespread story about losing his virginity to a goat. Despite having bowed legs of unequal length he became a Brazilian legend for the wing play that helped win the 1958 and 1962 World Cups. But behind the success was a boy from a very poor background who was working in a factory at 14. He was said to have slept with hundreds of women and fathered at least 14 children. He never confirmed or denied the goat story but he was a heavy drinker and was in a car crash that killed his mother-in-law. He died in an alcoholic coma aged 49 in 1983.

Cup match postponed 29 times

A Scottish Cup match scheduled for 6 January 1979 eventually took place on 22 February after 29 postponements. Bad weather hit Scotland in early January with Inverness Caledonian Thistle due to meet Falkirk in the second round of the cup. Try as they may, the weather beat all efforts to play the game and the pitch at Inverness was not playable until six weeks later. Falkirk's four goals in the first half saw them go through but because of the cup fixture congestion that had built up by this time, Falkirk were forced to play the next round within three days and lost to Dundee.

Football fails to weather the storms

More than 500 games had to be postponed in England and Scotland when prolonged Arctic conditions struck in the 1962–63 season. With sub-zero conditions persisting for weeks, 400 English league and cup games were postponed as were hundreds more in Scotland. The fixture congestion was so bad that the season on both sides of the border was, in an unprecedented move, extended by a month. In the FA Cup Coventry and Lincoln's third-round match was postponed 16 times and in the Scottish Cup Airdrie and Stranraer created a British record of 33 postponements.

Own worst enemy

Three players – Vince Kenny, Norman Curtis and Eddie Gannon – scored own goals as Sheffield Wednesday lost 5–4 to West Bromwich in a English First Division match.

Celebration becomes a bummer

A mass "mooning" joke by Wimbledon players had a price tag – £11,750. The London club's so-called "Crazy Gang" gathered to drop their shorts at the crowd during a testimonial for team-mate Alan Cork. The players were already on a high from two days before when they beat the favourites Liverpool to win the FA Cup and admitted that the interim before the testimonial had been a blur, courtesy of their beer-company sponsors. But egged on by their supporters, the players dropped their shorts, then stumped up £750 each in fines imposed by the English FA. Wimbledon was additionally fined £5,000.

Stay-away fans create dismal record

The lowest attendance for an international European game was in 1996 when just 200 people formed a crowd at Trabzon in Turkey as Azerbaijan and Poland produced a less-than-thrilling 0–0 draw in a Euro 96 qualifier. At European club level, Olympiakos Nicosia featured in two of the lowest attended Intertoto Cup matches. In a first-round tie in 2003 the club attracted 71 people against ZTS Dubnica from Slovakia and in 2005 bettered it by only nine against Gloria Bistrita of Romania.

Disgraceful first

Kevin Keegan and Billy Bremner became the first British players sent off at Wembley. The two staged a punch-up in a generally bad-tempered FA Charity Shield between Liverpool and Leeds, then compounded their offence by throwing their shirts on to the pitch.

"Noisy" neighbour

Premiership footballer Diego Arismendi was accused of forcing his neighbour to move because of an alleged string of noisy, late-night parties. Noisy indoor kickabout sessions were also cited in 2010 by plastic surgeon Dr Muhammad Khan who lived below the Uruguayan midfielder, 22, who was with Stoke City. The doctor claimed loud music that made his flat vibrate was played until 5 am, forcing him to hand in his notice for his rented luxury apartment. Arismendi denied the doctor's complaints.

Prison road to international stardom

Jamie Lawrence was put on the road to a much-travelled career because his football skills were spotted playing in a prison team in 1993. Within a year he was playing for Sunderland and went on to have a career involving 12 clubs and 24 international caps for Jamaica. The player, who was comfortable in midfield or defence, had been involved in crime as a youth living in London. In 1990 he received a four-year jail sentence for a bank robbery and that was when his talent for robbing opponents of the ball was spotted.

Jose's medals are a windfall for fans

Premier League medals awarded to coach Jose Mourinho when he was in England with Chelsea turned out to be a bonus for two fans. Mourinho celebrated Chelsea's championship win in 2006 by throwing his medals into the Stamford Bridge crowd as a thank you for the massive support of loyal fans who had taken the coach to their hearts. In 2008 one of the spectators who caught the first medal sold his for more than £21,000, while another hung on to his prize until 2010 before getting an estimated £15,000 at auction.

Miss, miss, miss

Three players missed the same penalty in an English league game between Notts County and Portsmouth in 1973. The kick for Notts County was retaken twice because of encroachment, but still no one hit the net.

Pele stops a war for a few hours

The famous Great War Christmas Day truce was not the only time that football had silenced guns. Pele and the great Santos team halted the slaughter in Nigeria's Biafran War in 1969. Although Nigerian federal troops were locked in a murderous campaign against the breakaway state of Biafra, Pele and his Santos team were on tour and were due to play two exhibition matches. With the populations of both warring sides soccer mad, truces were negotiated so that people could watch the brilliant Brazilians in action with all the tricks and flicks of the Samba tradition.

Was it FIFA's revenge on US "rebels"?

There were dark mutterings in US soccer circles over why the States did not stage the 1986 World Cup finals. Conspiracy theorists allege world football body FIFA was paying back the USA for previous transgressions. FIFA and the US Federation clashed in 1981 over the North American Soccer League (NASL) changing the offside line from halfway to 35 yards and employing shoot-outs to decide drawn matches. FIFA was not happy about rule changes it hadn't sanctioned, but the NASL threatened to go to court. Five years later, when it became obvious Colombia could not stage the 1986 finals, the US made a credible bid led by ace diplomat Henry Kissinger but FIFA rejected it in favour of Mexico who had staged the finals in 1970. The US had to wait another eight years.

Football hastens end of Yugoslavia

A football match that never happened has been credited with being the catalyst to the break-up of Yugoslavia. With Communism dying in the region in 1990, Red Star Belgrade of Serbia were due to play Dinamo Zagreb of Croatia at the time Croatian nationalists were getting their separatist campaign underway. Serbs in Red Star's hooligan fringe opposed to the federation split started a riot in Zagreb that took more than an hour to subdue and led to the game being called off. Within months Serbs and Croats were killing each other in a "Patriotic War" that ended in Croatian independence, but many Croats viewed the skirmishes at Zagreb's Maksimir Stadium as the first battle.

Excuse me

Although Dmitri Kramarenko was the best goalkeeper of his generation, he seemed loathe to play for Azerbaijan and was inventive with his excuses. They included "thieves stole my passport"; "I have strained something"; or "I have a family crisis". He still won 33 caps from 1992 to 2005.

Boring match?

A fan who nodded off in a Middlesbrough game in 2004 was ejected by stewards, fined £150 and had his season ticket revoked. He was accused of being drunk, but this was overturned on appeal and preserved the right of any fan to nod off in a boring draw.

Priest on the team

Birmingham City tried to change their on-the-pitch luck in 1980 by bringing in a priest to put a cross on the home dressing-room door and bless players' boots.

Half-time is for resigning and firing

Half-time might be a time for relaxing and regrouping for players but it can be a dodgy period for managers. Harald Schumacher was as controversial as a manager as he was a player and was even fired at half-time in 1999. He wasn't around to see his Fortuna Cologne team run out for the second half of a German second division game. With his side trailing 0–2 at home, club president Jean Loering fired Schumacher because he said the former German international goalkeeper had no idea about tactics and had confused his players. It seems they were even more confused going out managerless for the second half – as Schumacher packed his kit bag and left they succumbed 1–5.

Bad reputation goes back 700 years

England's King Edward II was no fan of football – in fact he banned it way back in 1314. With great prescience about what was to follow many centuries later, the King put the block on it being played because he feared it would cause social unrest – and even treason. Football in those days was unregulated mayhem with rival villages taking chunks out of each other fly-hacking a pig's bladder around rough ground. Edward's royal decree couldn't put a total stop to football's development, but he would be spinning in his grave if he could see a modern-day Arsenal–Manchester United affair.

Cup hero

Italian Football Federation secretary Ottorino Brassi kept the Jules Rimet World Cup trophy out of Nazi hands during World War 2 by hiding it under his bed and then in chicken coops. Italy had won the cup in 1938.

Cup meltdown

The original gold World Cup was stolen and melted down after Brazil was awarded permanent custody for their three tournament wins. Thieves took advantage of lax security to steal it from the Brazilian Federation offices in Rio de Janeiro.

Preston – hellraisers of 1880s

Trouble seemed to follow Preston North End around in the early days of organised English football. Both the players and the supporters proved they could handle themselves in violent situations. In 1885 a North End 5–0 demolition of Aston Villa in a friendly made Villa fans distinctly unfriendly. They surrounded the Preston team with violence in mind, but the Preston players put up a great fight even though one of their number was knocked unconscious. Several years later police had to be called to break up fights between Preston supporters and those of Scottish club Queen's Park. Later still, a 70-year-old woman was counted among Preston fans tried for hooliganism and drunkenness.

Zerouali is glad to be a zero

Moroccan striker Hicham Zerouali became the only player ever to wear the squad number zero in Scottish football. Aberdeen, his club between 1999 and 2002, gave him permission to sport the zero because that was Zerouali's nickname. But it lasted only a season before the Scottish Football Association ruled against it. Zerouali moved back to his native Morocco and was killed in a car accident aged 27 in 2004.

Partners and players

Iceland seems to be the place for perfect football marriages – where both partners excel. Between 1992 and 1995 Haraldur Ingolfsson, who played briefly in Scotland with Aberdeen, and his wife Jonina Viglundsdottir both won international caps for Iceland. Hermann Hreidarsson, who was with Portsmouth in 2010, and fellow centre back and wife Ragna Loa Stefansdottir also both have a big collection of Iceland caps between them. Of Swedish couple Hans Eskilsson and Malin Swedberg, it was Malin who was the most successful at international level. She represented her country 78 times while Hans had just eight caps.

All change

Leeds United players, who were angrily surrounding referee Ray Tinkler to remonstrate over a disputed goal, had to suddenly become his protectors as a crowd of angry fans rushed to join in during an English First Division game.

Records tumble in amazing comeback

There was just one team in it for an hour when Charlton Athletic met Huddersfield Town in an English Second Division match in 1957. With half an hour to go Huddersfield were 5–1 up. A fight-back led by winger Johnny Summers began and soon he had a club record of five goals in a match as Charlton led 6–5. Although stunned, Huddersfield made it 6–6 but, with the last kick of the match, Summers laid on a goal for John Ryan and Charlton's comeback was completed at 7–6. It brought an unwanted record for Huddersfield, the only team to score six goals and still end up on the losing side.

FA Cup winner on murder charge

A former Everton player ended up on a murder charge in Australia in the early years of the 20th century. Sandy Young won the 1906 FA Cup with Everton and after spells with Tottenham Hotspur and Manchester City he emigrated to Australia where in 1915 he was charged with the wilful murder of his brother. The following year he was found guilty of manslaughter instead and imprisoned for three years. He escaped the hangman's noose because evidence was obtained from English football authorities of Young's fits of temporary insanity. After serving his time, Young was kept in custody for "mental weakness" for some years before returning, it is believed, to his native Scotland.

Four for Chris

Any player would be happy to score four goals in a match but not Chris Nicholl of Aston Villa in 1976. His four included two own goals in a 2–2 draw with Leicester.

Zamorano adds up to a protest

The number was up for Chilean international Ivan Zamorano when Ronaldo was transferred from Barcelona to Inter Milan in 1997. Zamorano didn't fear that the Brazilian striker would take his place in the side – more that his squad number 9 would go to him. Ronaldo always played in the classic centre forward number but when he moved to Inter Milan Zamorano was the holder. Despite his protestations, the weight of Ronaldo's reputation won through and he got the 9. A furious Zamorano made his feelings known by wearing a shirt sporting 1+8 as a protest.

Liverpool's tartan army

With 21st-century football truly international, clubs fielding a side comprising all foreign players is not unusual. When Liverpool did it in 1892 it caused a stir because they put out a complete team of Scots for their first competitive match. The phenomenon came against the background of the split in the original Liverpool club, which led to players breaking away to form Everton. Manager John McKenna ended doubts over whether Liverpool FC could find enough players by recruiting all 11 players from the city's Scottish community.

Wakey wakey, it's time to kick off

Barcelona staged a match with a 12.05 am kick-off in a bid to fit in a game before their stars left for international duty. Barca wanted to play a midweek fixture against Sevilla with a full-strength squad before an international weekend in September 2003. International players had to be released four days before but Sevilla refused to move the fixture to allow Barca's stars to play. With the exception of Portugal, the countries expecting their Barcelona-based internationals also refused to go along with Barca's plan. But such is Barcelona's support that 80,000 people still turned out at midnight to see a 1–1 draw.

Secret resignation

Don Revie resigned as England manager in 1977 but didn't tell his bosses at the English FA until after they read it as an exclusive in a national newspaper. After a mediocre record with England he managed the United Arab Emirates national squad.

Politics vs football

Soviet football legend Oleh Blokhin had to choose between political and football coaching careers. The Dinamo Kiev striker was a Communist member of the Ukrainian Parliament in 2003 when he was appointed national football coach. He resigned when political opponents claimed the two roles were incompatible and it was illegal to hold both. The case went to court and a judge ruled for Blokhin who guided Ukraine to 2006 World Cup qualification.

China bids to make football impact

A Chinese youth team was sent away from home for five years in 1993 to get a football education from the best in the world, Brazil. Keen to develop a top-class football culture that would stand the country in good stead in future, Chinese authorities sent the young Jianlibao team to soak up the football atmosphere in Brazil, and it worked because several of the players went on to play in top leagues. Later, a two-year training camp in Germany produced the nucleus for a China side in the Beijing Olympics.

Frank-ly out of luck

Frank Haffey was a late call-up as Scotland's goalkeeper against England in 1961. By the end of the match he must have wished he hadn't pulled on the jersey because England treated a packed Wembley Stadium to a 9–3 win. Haffey never played for his country again.

Brazil referees draw the line

The vexed question of how to enforce the 10-yard rule for defensive walls at free kicks seemed to have been solved in Brazil in 2000. A chemist came up with a biodegradable, non-toxic aerosol spray with which referees could draw a line for the defence. The line stays for around a minute, giving just enough time for the kick to be taken. Widely adopted in Brazilian football, FIFA seemed unimpressed by the innovation and ten years on had yet to rule on taking it up worldwide.

Code switch clinches Super Bowl win

Austrian international Toni Fritsch may not have won much at association soccer but he was a world-beater at American football. He remains the only Austrian ever to win a Super Bowl. Best known for scoring two goals in a historic Austrian 3–2 win over England in 1965, he was signed up as a specialist goal kicker for the Dallas Cowboys with whom he won a Super Bowl in 1972. Fritsch had 12 seasons in American football with various teams.

Loser takes all

Amsterdam's Ajax club won the KNVB Cup in 1970. This is not a surprising statement for one of the Netherlands' legendary and most-successful clubs but it was unusual because they were knocked out earlier. They lost in the last 16 to AZ Alkmaar but because of an irregularity there had only been 15 in the round. It meant that one of the seven losers was reprieved with Ajax given a second chance they grasped with both hands, beating PSV Eindhoven 2–0 in the final.

Ahoy there

Supporters of two English clubs staged their own sea battle in 1986 when they clashed on a ferry taking them to Europe. West Ham and Manchester United fans fought with bottles, knives and fire hoses on a Harwich–Hook of Holland ferry – it was taking them to friendly matches on the continent.

Politics put Israel in Europe

Decades of Middle East tension and the state of war that exists between Israel and its neighbours has led to the country moving to Europe in football terms. During the 1990s Israel was accepted into UEFA and its clubs now compete in the European Champions League and Europa League, while the national team attempts to qualify for the World Cup finals against European opposition. Technically, Israel should be with neighbours such as Syria, Jordan and Lebanon among others in the Asian Football Confederation but prior to 1991 were not given the opportunity to compete in regional club competitions because of the political and security issues.

Non-league side face England

Aylesbury United remain the only non-league side to face a full England international team. The "Ducks" from Buckinghamshire were the reigning Beazer Homes Southern League champions in 1988 when they provided the opposition for the final England warm-up game before Euro 88. Only around 6,000 people saw England thrash Aylesbury 7–0 and Peter Beardsley hit four of them. Unfortunately, when England got to West Germany the goal touch deserted them and they lost all three group matches for a quick return home.

Cayman Islands loophole that failed

The Cayman Islands' attempt to end their football obscurity in 2000 was a failure. As a British dependent territory, the local FA thought it could recruit better players from Britain as long as they held British passports. A number of players from lower leagues in England and Scotland were recruited and lost a friendly with the USA. However, FIFA stepped in against the possible loophole before the Caymans could face a World Cup 2002 qualifier against Cuba and the British players were sent home. FIFA said players had to be five-year residents of the islands, Cayman born or with Cayman descendants.

Rough for Clough

Outspoken but fair-minded manager Brian Clough lambasted his own Nottingham Forest supporters for their abuse of rival striker Charlie George. Clough charged from his dugout to remonstrate with them for jeering as the Arsenal man was stretchered off.

Cindy wins 100 caps – at 23

The youngest player to achieve a century of caps for their country is a woman. USA international striker Cindy Parlow was just 23 years, one month and 26 days when in a friendly against Canada in 2001 she appeared for the 100th time for the USA. Parlow, also the youngest person to win Olympic football gold and women's World Cup medals, retired from the US international scene in 2006 with 158 caps and 75 goals under her belt.

Broken China

Thousands of rioting fans took to the streets of Chinese capital Beijing in 1985 after the Republic's team lost a World Cup qualifier 2–1 to British-run colony Hong Kong.

Steve's TV revenge

Liverpool captain Steven Gerrard got his revenge on a TV presenter who said on air that the midfielder was overweight. Feigning anger Gerrard rang Colin Murray from Channel 4's *RI:SE* programme and gave him a convincing-sounding ear bashing down the phone. He kept Murray going for a bit before revealing the joke.

Room-mates fall out

1970 World Cup England squad room-mates Francis Lee and Norman Hunter violently fell out five years later when playing for their clubs. They not only fought on the pitch, but also continued to attack each other on the way to the dressing room in a disgraceful show at a Derby County–Leeds United game. Lee had a reputation for diving to get penalties and on this day upset hard man Hunter when he won a soft penalty. Behind the ref's back Hunter took his retribution and gave Lee a split lip, but other players saw everything and pitched in, leading to Hunter and Lee's dismissal. As they left the field, Lee snapped under Hunter's goading and floored the much taller Leeds man.

Signing new wingers

An investment in new "wingers" was a money-saving plan for Fulham in 2012. The West London club bought a dozen chickens in a bid to slash its food bill. With its players getting through 90 eggs a day, the club reckoned its new "signings" would save £5,000 a year.

Reffing old

Doug Milton, Britain's oldest referee, was still turning out for local league games in Surrey during 2009 – at the age of 90.

Bum rap

Northern Ireland full back Sammy Nelson was fined and suspended by Arsenal for dropping his shorts and showing his backside to fans. He had equalised for Arsenal but had been barracked by the crowd for giving Coventry the lead with an own goal.

Boss in disgrace

Graeme Souness was sent off in his first match as the new player-manager of Glasgow Rangers in 1986. His lunging tackle injured Hibernian striker George McCluskey and sparked a mass fight among players.

Missed career

Daddy was right for the 6th Duke of Westminster. His father disliked the trend of kissing other men and forbade a football career. The one-time Fulham trialist instead became 20th-century Britain's third richest man, owning huge tracts of London and Paris.

That kiss

The first pictured kiss on a football pitch circulated around the world within hours. Pals and on-pitch rivals Alan Birchenall of Leicester City and Tony Currie of Sheffield United had, after a tackle, found themselves seated face to face on the grass. The duo puckered up – and the rest is photographic history.

Driller killer

A spot of do-it-yourself surgery with a power drill landed former England striker Darius Vassell in hospital. During his time with Aston Villa in 2003 he picked up an infection after attempting to drain a blood blister with a power drill. It led to the forward having part of a toenail removed.

Fan proves his point

Critical fan Steve Davies ended up putting his skills where his mouth was. Watching his beloved West Ham play Oxford in a 1994 pre-season friendly, Davies was so incensed at the ineptitude of the Hammers' performance he poured a tirade of abuse on the hapless team. West Ham assistant manager Harry Redknapp finally lost patience with Davies' barracking and challenged him that if he could do better he should get into the claret and blue strip and prove it. In the 30 minutes he was given on the pitch he did do better and actually scored.

Hair-pulling squabble shames players

If anyone had thought that the histrionics and Alice bands of the modern game had given footballers a "girly" image, it was confirmed in August 2009 when two Swiss league players resorted to a hair-pulling scuffle. Basel goalkeeper Franco Costanzo got into an argument with defender Beg Ferati who pushed the Argentinian away. This further enraged Costanzo who grabbed Ferati by his hair until team-mates separated them. The hair-raising incident was in a 1–1 draw with FC Zurich that was televised to millions of Swiss soccer fans. Costanzo was fined.

Everybody off – almost

Two players were left on the pitch when a referee went on a red-card spree in 1993. He dished out 20 reds during a game between Sportivo Ameliano and General Caballero in Paraguay. After two Sportivo players were dismissed, a ten-minute fight ensued and the ref sent off a further 18 and abandoned the match.

Victory parade ends in disaster

Many of the players who helped win promotion for Brazilian club Sertaozinho were injured as they celebrated their success in 2005. Not having the traditional double-decker bus handy, the team piled on top of a loudspeaker truck to tour the streets of Sao Paulo. Although the truck had side rails, putting over a ton of players' and officials' weight at the very top altered its centre of gravity. At a dip in the road the entire team were thrown off. There were no deaths or career-threatening injuries among the people pitched to the ground and most of the injuries were broken limbs.

Sick as a genuine parrot

Referees are used to getting the bird from fans, but not from the real thing. English referee Gary Bailey was baffled by a repeated whistling that kept stopping play in a Hertfordshire County FA Cup between Hatfield and Hertford Heath in 1995. His investigation led him to the culprit, not 66-year-old spectator Irene Kerrigan – but her parrot Me-Tu whom she had brought to the game for some fresh air. Bailey promptly gave the feathered whistling menace a straight red and Me-Tu and Irene were sent packing. In true Arnie Schwarzenegger fashion though, Irene and parrot promised they would be back.

Flip-flop fiasco makes Gattuso see red

Being called off the bench to take part in a match came as a surprise to AC Milan's Clarence Seedorf in a 2009 Milan derby match. When the call came with Inter Milan 4–0 up, the Dutchman was just chilling on the bench – and wearing flip-flops. This inability to be prepared to come on as a substitute contributed to the dismissal of captain Rene Gattuso who was the injured player, already on a yellow card, waiting to come off. Needing several minutes to get into shin-pads, socks and boots, Seedorf forced Gattuso to stay on the field for what proved to be a disastrous extra few minutes. In that time Gattuso, a full-blooded player, chopped down Wesley Sneijder and was red-carded. Furious with Seedorf, Gattuso stormed off in a rage.

Manager gagged

The FA barred England manager Bobby Robson from writing a column for money in a national newspaper in 1986. It said if the manager had views they should be shared with all media.

Zara bids to save daddy's job

A 13-year-old girl made an impassioned national plea to save her father's job as England manager. Glenn Hoddle was in hot water in 1999 over comments he had made about disabled people paying for their sins in a previous life. Although the Hoddle claimed he was misquoted it caused a furore and, fearing the worst for her dad, Zara Hoddle contacted the TV-based national information service Ceefax to drum up some support for him. She wrote: "I am very supportive of disabled people, so is my dad, but this is the most pathetic reason for someone to have maybe lost their job and to have so much hassle over." Despite her plea Hoddle was fired.

Meredith's 100-year-shirt legacy

A Manchester United strip designed in 1909 by a player earning £4 a week earned the club millions in replica sales a century later. The iconic V-style shirts were reintroduced by the English Premiership champions and manufacturer Nike in 2009 – and as with all new strip designs admiring fans spent millions on it. The original V-strip was designed a century before by "Welsh Wizard" winger Billy Meredith, who ironically earned the equivalent, at 2009 prices, of £298 a year as a star United player. No wonder that fiery Meredith championed higher wages for professional players. Meredith got nothing for his design, which was in non-traditional white with a red shoulder-to-shoulder V.

Seventh hell

Billy Minter scored seven goals in a match – and finished on the losing side. His superb solo FA Cup performance was for St Albans City in 1922, but Dulwich Hamlet beat them 8–7.

Romania desperate for a winning spell

When a Communist government threatens reprisals for a defeat, you pull out all the stops – even resorting to sorcery. The Romanians went as far as witchcraft to try to secure a much-needed victory. Tyrannical president Nicolae Ceausescu's government demanded in 1989 nothing short of victory by the Romanian team over Denmark and threatened to sack the whole of the football federation, the national team and their manager. Federation president Mircea Sandu hired a witch to put a spell on Danish captain and goalkeeper Peter Schmeichel. Whether the witch's powers were successfully all-powerful or Schmeichel's side had an off day is unclear, but Romania staved off the threat with a 3–1 win.

L'amour in song for beleaguered boss

Former porn actress Catherine Ringer distracted French coach Raymond Domenech from the criticism of his reign with the national side by penning a song of love. The under-fire France boss received a vocal vote of confidence from her as his side struggled to reach the finals of the 2010 World Cup in South Africa. The saucy songstress released a CD called "Je Kiffe Raymond" ("I Fancy Raymond"), with several touching couplets about the former Paris St Germain midfield hard man. Domenech attracted media criticism as his side struggled and needed Thierry Henry's double handball against the Republic of Ireland to save France's World Cup campaign.

Maradona explodes

Argentina coach Diego Maradona launched a foul-mouthed tirade at the media that had criticised his country's stuttering 2010 World Cup qualifying campaign. "You lot take it up the arse," were Diego Maradona's words to the press immediately after his team secured the last qualifying place in the South America group for the World Cup finals. He continued: "But certain people who have not supported me, and you know who you are, can keep sucking."

Putting some bite into the tackles

Three players were bitten when a fleeing police dog ran amok in an amateur game in England in 2002. The German Shepherd had escaped from his handler during an exercise at a disused building close to the pitch at Scunthorpe in Lincolnshire. It first snatched a linesman's flag before attacking players Craig Jackson, 18, Steve Baker, 19, and Michael Stones, 18. They were bitten on the arms and back and were treated at hospital; the game between Appleby Frodingham and Lincoln Moorlands was abandoned.

Stan lights them up

In an early example of star endorsement, super-fit non-smoker Sir Stanley Matthews leant his name to a cigarette brand in the 1950s. Adverts attributed his "smooth ball control" to the "smoothness" of Craven A.

Gone west

Nigerian international Taribo West was sacked by German club Kaiserslautern for missing a game to celebrate his 28th birthday in 2002. There was not a drink in sight at his "party", which was a six-hour Christian evangelical meeting.

Name games

The Arsenal dropped its "The" and became simply "Arsenal" because 1930´s manager Herbert Chapman wanted the club to head the list of First Division clubs.

Whistle takes a bow

Previous to the whistle being introduced in 1878, referees waved a handkerchief to command games.

Drink up and be my guest

A touch of genius won Peter Guest beer for life in his local pub in Somerset. Guest was going to the World Cup finals in Japan and South Korea in 2002 and Martin Smith, who runs the Bull Inn where Guest enjoys a pint, promised him free booze if he could get the pub's name on TV. And he did it. Guest took a banner with the pub's name and address on it, along with a hello message for his wife Jenny, to the England–Denmark game and it appeared on screen ten times. Despite losing the bet, the landlord was thrilled to see his pub's name in front of millions across the world.

Good, bad and ugly

In the space of just five minutes Barnsley striker Ashley Ward scored, missed a penalty and was sent off in a 1998 game at Sunderland.

Short break

A piece of elastic may have had a profound effect on Italy's 1938 World Cup win – but for the cool head of Giuseppe Meazza. In the semi-final his shorts fell down as he was taking a penalty against Brazil but, holding his shorts up, he calmly slotted the ball home.

Pig-headed fan is barred

A pig got a red card before it even got in to see a top-level Russian league match. Its owner was barred from taking it into a 2009 Zenit St Petersburg game with Spartak Moscow in case it incited a riot. Farmer and football fan Vladimir Kisilev from St Petersburg took his prize-winning pig to a show in Moscow and wanted to watch a national Premier League match while he was in the Russian capital. Unfortunately, he had nowhere to leave the beast and tried to get it into the ground. Police banned the pig although, but for an inopportune grunt, it might have made it. Kisilev said: "I almost managed to get it through in a big bag but it started grunting and the police noticed."

Thunderstruck

Italian legend Luigi Riva was nicknamed "Thunder" for his powerful shots and once broke the arm of a spectator with an off-target drive.

"Cops and robbers" show is a winner

Although a 1975 English First Division league match between Southampton and Norwich City was not great for fans, the half-time entertainment was riveting. There was to be a police dog display at the interval with a hooded figure running on to the pitch shouting and firing a gun into the air pursued by a German Shepherd police dog ready to pounce. However, an overenthusiastic constable on safety control duty in the ground had not been briefed. As the crowd at Southampton's The Dell roared with laughter the PC, believing the situation to be real, hared across the field, rugby tackled the "pretend" assailant and arrested him, leaving the bewildered dog with nothing to do. The PC sheepishly put his helmet back on and returned to duty but was later seen signing autographs.

Opposition fans were wary of Waring

There was no messing about with Tom "Pongo" Waring, a no-nonsense Aston Villa striker – in more ways than one – during the 1930s. Although much revered for his scoring skills he added legendary status with Aston Villa supporters in a game at Villa Park. Waring had gone to fetch the ball, which had gone out of play, when he heard someone shout an insulting remark. Waring dropped the ball, waded into the crowd and punched the offender. He then received a rapturous round of applause when he returned to the pitch. He was neither sent off, nor punished by his club or the Football Association and, unlike today, was not charged by the police.

Strong-arm Armstrong

Northern Ireland international Gerry Armstrong took the law into his own hands when he heard disparaging remarks from the crowd while playing for Brighton and Hove Albion in a Sussex Cup tie in 1988. He clambered into the stands and headbutted Wayne Marmont, who required six stitches in a gashed forehead. Armstrong was charged with grievous bodily harm and was red-carded for the first time in his career. In court the Ulsterman was conditionally discharged for a year and ordered to pay £200 compensation and £20 costs. He left Brighton under something of a cloud.

Quick-fire mood

James Hayter proved an inspired substitution when he came on in the 84th minute for Bournemouth and scored the fastest English Football League hat-trick – under 140 seconds – against Wrexham. His parents missed it as they had to leave the match early.

The United States of Ire-merica

One of the features that has developed with the USA's Major League Soccer (MLS) is supporters' ability to inflame players. Several players have clashed with fans including David Beckham, who confronted highly vocal and highly critical Los Angeles Galaxy fans in 2008. Clint Mathis was fined $500 for something similar in 2003, although neither involved physical violence. In 2001 Tampa Bay's Mamadou Diallo, the MLS's top goalscorer for 2000, threw a punch at a Colorado Rapids' fan as he walked off the pitch at full-time following a 2–1 defeat. The Rapids fan, whom Senegalese Diallo accused of racial abuse, apparently needed the help of an umbrella to fend off the attacker. However, the incident earned Diallo a four-game suspension.

Sharp lesson for failures

The price of defeat was higher than expected for 11 players from the Burkina Faso army side, Armed Forces Sporting Union, in the 1998–99 season. The team members had their heads shaved and were thrown into jail for the night after losing a decisive game. The club's hard-line president, Commander Zoumana Traore, explained his actions: "It's true that it was only football but the people concerned must realise that they are soldiers and playing football in the army is not simply sport but is a mission. If I had them shaved it is to show that every time they have to defend the army's honour they must undertake their task with all seriousness."

Torture – the price of failure in Iraq

Not even sport was immune from the horrors of the Saddam Hussein regime in Iraq during the 1980s and 1990s. The dictator's equally sadistic son Uday was in charge of the national team and handed out inhuman punishments as the price of failure. They included beatings and being forced to kick a concrete ball. Former player Sharar Haydar recounted that after a friendly match defeat to Jordan he and three team-mates were hauled to prison, tied to bars and then dragged over concrete, tearing the skin off their backs. They then were made to jump into a vat of raw sewage to infect their wounds. In addition, as star player, Haydar was given 20 lashes a day.

Definite "no"

What a difference four days makes. On 1 June 2009 AC Milan star Kaka said: "I say it for the last time, I don't want to leave." On 6 June 2009 Brazilian-born Kaka moved to Real Madrid for a then world record £68.5m.

Star recruit

A lowly English club reached the semi-finals of the 2001 FA Cup with the help of British TV information service Ceefax. Injury-hit Wycombe Wanderers faced Leicester City in the quarter-finals without a recognised front man and put a plea for help on Ceefax. Roy Essandoh was recruited and headed a dramatic late winner.

Anthem provokes Muslim protests

A verse, which mysteriously appeared in an anthem sung by fans of the German club FC Schalke 04, caused furious protests from Muslims in 2009. They complained about a reference to the Prophet Muhammad and an expert on Islam was called to consider whether the song might be insulting. FC Schalke 04 from Gelsenkirchen received hundreds of e-mails after Turkish media uncovered the verse. It is believed the song was written in 1924 and it is unclear when the Muhammad reference made its way in.

Poseur gatecrashes United's party

Manchester United fan Karl Power was immortalised in an official team picture with his idols because he found a loophole in their security. In 2001 Power, an unemployed labourer from Greater Manchester, evaded security at Bayern Munich's Olympic Stadium to walk out with the Reds, before cheekily posing alongside the likes of Dwight Yorke, Ryan Giggs and Fabian Barthez. Eagle-eyed Gary Neville spotted the impostor and pointed him out to the rest of the team. It was reported that Power, a big Eric Cantona fan, told him: "Shut it, I'm doing this for Eric." Power has since done the same at other major sporting events.

Fan wrecks Denmark Euro 2008 bid

A single hothead was blamed for Denmark failing to qualify for Euro 2008. With a 2007 qualifier with Scandinavian rivals Sweden delicately poised at 3–3, the Danes were reduced to ten men after midfielder Christian Poulsen was dismissed for punching Sweden's Markus Rosenberg. Sweden were also awarded a penalty and at this point a Danish fan, incensed by the perceived injustice, ran on to the field. He aimed a punch at German referee Helmut Fandel, who immediately abandoned the game. The match was later awarded as a 3–0 win to Sweden, who went on to the Euro 2008 finals; Denmark failed to qualify.

Barefoot star wins over Celtic fans

An Indian-born player who had only ever played in bare feet was temporarily snapped up by Scottish club Glasgow Celtic in 1937. Because everyone else on the field was in boots Mohammed Salim played in bandaged feet and still impressed the then Celtic manager, Willie Maley, who agreed to give him a trial. Proving to be a skilful winger, Salim made his debut in 1937 and helped Celtic win 5–1 against Galston. In his second game Celtic beat Hamilton Academicals 7–0. Despite fan and media excitement about his skills Salim, nicknamed "The Indian Juggler", returned to India and died in poverty – his dream of a professional career unfulfilled.

Load of balls

Defender Liviu Baicea moved between Romanian clubs Jiul Petrosani to UT Arad in 1998 – the fee was ten footballs.

Dons offal prospect of big defeat

Controversial Wimbledon FC owner of the 1980s and 1990s, Sam Hammam, reportedly wrote some bizarre clauses into players' contracts. One was said to stipulate that if the Dons lost a game by five clear goals, Hammam could force the squad to attend an opera and eat offal-based dishes at a Lebanese restaurant. Robbie Earle, the Wimbledon captain of the time, said: "It was all in writing. If we lost by five clear goals, Sam could make us eat a meal which has to include sheep's testicles and all sorts of brains, intestines and horrible-sounding stuff." The threat seemed to work for the squad, known as the "Crazy Gang", never lost by the stated margin although they did come close, losing 5–1 to Arsenal in 1999.

Ref loses control – of himself

A referee gave himself a red card for attacking a player. He admitted the red mist came down during an English non-league fixture and after being pushed in the back and sworn at by the player the ref blew his top and punched him several times. The official then sent himself off and a spectator took charge of the remainder of the game. The referee was later fined £20 and banned for six weeks. Annoyed at the punishment said after the verdict: "The disciplinary committee got their priorities all wrong. They've convicted me of assault but the circumstances have not been shown. They've taken the side of the player, I was sorely provoked."

Off, off, off, off

Scottish club Stranraer created a record in 1994 of having four players sent off in a single match. With seven men they went from a 1–0 lead to a 1–8 defeat against Airdrie.

Judge lifts lid on player sex scandal

John Terry was sacked as England captain after his extra-marital love life was revealed in January 2010. A High Court judge lifted an injunction gagging media coverage of his affair with French lingerie model Vanessa Perroncel. It came months after Terry was voted "Dad of the Year" by a well-known sauce brand in Britain. It was alleged that Terry had cheated on his wife Toni with a long-term affair with Perroncel while she was the lover of Terry's good friend and England squad colleague Wayne Bridge.

Clapped out

Demanding Real Madrid fans were not happy with David Beckham for a 2005 defeat in which he stupidly got sent off. Having already been yellow-carded for dissent, the former England captain sarcastically applauded referee Arturo Dauden Ibanez and earned himself a second yellow.

Vital goal for striker

Italian striker Alessandro Del Piero has scored more than 200 goals in his professional career but none was more vital than the off-field goal he set himself – to help a 12-year-old girl come out of a coma. Football-mad Giada Scalise suffered a brain haemorrhage in February 2012 while watching her beloved Juventus – and Del Piero – on TV. When he learned of Giada's plight the striker recorded video and audio messages which were played to her in hospital in Crotone, Italy. In March 2012, Giada woke from her coma, a miracle attributed by the girl's father Francesco to the 37-year-old Italian international.

Ave Maria

After Sampdoria staved off relegation from Italy's Serie A in 1969, the team and 200 supporters walked 20 miles to a mountain sanctuary near Genoa to thank the Virgin Mary.

Drinking in his success – too much

England and Arsenal defender Tony Adams was jailed in 1990 for four months after he was found in his crashed car more than four times over Britain's legal drink-drive limit. After his sentence was handed down Adams was handcuffed to another prisoner who is said to have groaned in dismay because he was a fan of Arsenal's bitter north London rivals, Tottenham Hotspur. Despite being revealed as an alcoholic there were other drink-related incidents including falling downstairs at home and needing 29 stitches to a head wound. Adams later started the Sporting Chance Clinic dedicated to helping sportsmen and women with a variety of addictions and behavioural problems.

Three die in Togo team attack

Three people died when the Togo national team bus was attacked on its way to the 2010 Africa Cup of Nations tournament in Angola. None of the team was killed but several were injured when the bus came under automatic gunfire in an attack that lasted 20 minutes. The Front for the Liberation of the Enclave of Cabinda (FLEC) was blamed for the ambush. With several players traumatised by the incident, Togo withdrew from the competition. The Confederation of African Football (CAF) responded with an appalling lacking of sympathy by announcing that Togo was to be banned from the next two Africa Cup of Nations and fined $50,000 because of their withdrawal.

Blacked out and seeing red

A player was red-carded by a referee as he was stretchered off unconscious and taken to hospital in 2012. Julien Lecomte of Hainaut provincial side RSC Templeuvois in Belgium was eventually diagnosed with three displaced vertebrae and concussion but was sent off because the ref reckoned he dived. Lecomte was playing against USG Quevy 89 when he was elbowed in the neck and landed badly in the penalty area, but the referee decided that the player had tried to hoodwink him into giving a spot kick. Ten-man Templeuvois lost 2-1 but remained second in the table, while USG climbed to fifth.

Seconds out

A 1991 match halted by rioting was resumed for 35 seconds. Birmingham City fans had invaded the pitch after a Stoke City equaliser and, rather than abandon the game, the managers agreed to wait until the ground was cleared before playing out the last 35 seconds with the two sides tapping the ball to each other.

Memory lapse costs Ferdinand dear

Rio Ferdinand will always remember the day in 2003 when he forgot to turn up for a drugs test. Instead of staying on at Manchester United's Carrington training ground for the random UK Sport test, he headed for the shops to pick out curtains. It was an expensive shopping trip because Ferdinand, the United and England centre half, was banned from playing by the Football Association for eight months, fined £50,000 and had to pay the cost of the disciplinary hearing. The ban also ruled him out of England's appearances at Euro 2004.

Boro relegated by flu bug

The consequence of calling off a match through sickness was costly for Middlesbrough in the English Premier League in 1996. Faced with a flu epidemic that raged through the first team at Christmas, Boro decided not to take a side of "kids and crocks" to their away match in Blackburn. Despite their opponents' ire for not turning up at all, Boro chief executive Keith Lamb said the decision was the right one – until the end of the season came. Having been docked three points by the FA for failing to fulfil a fixture and reducing that by one with a drawn re-arranged game, Boro were relegated by two points.

Plea for fine time

A millionaire player asked for three weeks to stump up a mere £1,300 after a court case in 2010. The player, on a reported £100,000 a week, was fined £1,000 with £300 costs by magistrates. His lawyer begged for time to pay and got 21 days' grace. The player was also banned from driving for four months after his car was clocked at twice the legal limit – 104mph in a 50mph zone. He claimed he was trying to escape a chasing pack of paparazzi.

Dogged by pet

If it had happened on the pitch Liam Lawrence's pet dog would have received a yellow card. In 2010 the Stoke City midfielder's dog tripped him up and badly sprained his ankle during the player's late night visit to the bathroom.

212

Scotland's first World Cup debacle

Scotland's first World Cup appearance was dogged by problems in1954. The squad arrived in Switzerland without training gear because their Football Association had forgotten to pack it. While the team played in scrounged ill-matched gear it was discovered that the pennant to exchange in the first game with Austria was also forgotten. If the team was already demoralised then things were to get worse. They ended bottom of their group and failed to score a goal. Then, before a record 7–0 hammering by Uruguay, coach Andy Beattie resigned during his pre-match briefing.

Political game plan misfires

A political decision by the German FA led to the worst team ever appearing in the country's Bundesliga. With Hertha Berlin relegated in 1965 for irregularities, there was no team from the former capital in the top division so they promoted the totally unprepared Tasmania 1900 Berlin from division two. It soon became obvious that this was backfiring as Tasmania began collecting records for all the wrong reasons. They won just two games in the 1965–66 season; scored just eight points; lost one game 0–9; and in one match attracted a record low crowd of 827. Having also conceded 108 goals and scored a measly 15, they sunk without trace.

Press man is the cup hero

Glasgow Rangers' 1971-72 European Cup Winners' Cup campaign was saved by a sports reporter who was more diligent about the rules than the referee in the second leg of the quarter-final against Sporting Lisbon. With the aggregate scores at 6–6 the ref signalled a penalty shoot-out, which Rangers lost. It was then that the reporter got a message to the Rangers' manager Willie Waddell that the ref had not applied the new away goals rule. Rangers, who had won their home first leg 3-2, had scored three away goals in their 4-3 second leg defeat. Rangers, instead of being eliminated, went through and won the trophy.

Acting the goat

Manchester City's Shaun Goater celebrated team-mate Nicolas Anelka's goal in a 2003 match enthusiastically by kicking an advertising hoarding. He injured his knee and had to be subbed.

Returning Hogan's sock shock

Former Burnley and Bolton player Jimmy Hogan was furious to have been branded virtually a traitor in 1919 when he returned from internment during World War 1. He had been coaching in Austria when he was trapped by the onset of the 1914–18 war but was allowed to carry on working at his trade in Hungary. On his return he tried to claim the £200 for former players disadvantaged by the war and was sent three pairs of socks by the Football Association with a note saying: "The boys at the front were glad of these." He never got over the slight and moved back to central Europe where he became one of the region's most influential coaches.

By the book

Sir Stanley Matthews, who played for Stoke City and Blackpool, never received a booking in his 33-year career. He was 50 when he retired from top-class football.

Premature death

English non-league team Congleton called off a minute's silence to mourn the death of the club's oldest fan in 1993 because he had walked into the ground

White horse Billy saves big day

The first FA Cup final to be staged at Wembley was saved – by a white horse. With no risk assessments done in those days, 200,000 people crammed into a new stadium with a capacity of 125,000. The result was a potentially dangerous situation even though the crowds spilling on to the pitch were good-natured. Enter Pc George Scorey of the Metropolitan Police on his white horse Billy. With fears that the match between Bolton Wanderers and West Ham United would never take place Billy, joined by other less distinctively coloured police horses, spent 45 minutes nudging the crowd back. The subsequently named "White Horse Final" eventually started with the crowds crammed up to the touchline for Bolton to win 2–0.

Unlucky 13

Sheffield Wednesday goalkeeper Kevin Pressman was dismissed after just 13 seconds of the first game of the 2000–01 English league season.

Scotland bans boozy losers

Two Scottish internationals were barred for life from playing for their country in 2009 after an all-night drinking session while on international duty. Glasgow Rangers team-mates, midfielder Barry Ferguson and goalkeeper Allan McGregor, were axed from Scotland's starting line-up for the World Cup qualifier against Iceland following a late-night drinking session after the defeat in Holland a few days before. The pair compounded their offences by sitting in the stands at the Iceland game making surreptitious V signs. Both were also punished by their club and Ferguson, arguably the outstanding Scottish midfielder of his generation, was sold to Birmingham City.

Eighty die

Overcrowded stands were blamed for a crush that killed 80 and injured more than 200 at a 1997 World Cup qualifier against Honduras in Guatemala City. Many of the victims were children crushed and smothered amid the overcrowding.

United's 3D revolution

Manchester United, one of the world's premier clubs, was ahead of the game by being in the first live broadcast of a match in 3D. The 3D broadcast of United's vital Premiership match with Arsenal was seen by only a few hundred supporters in nine secret locations in 2010. Wearing special 3D glasses they saw United triumph 3–1 and feedback was positive. One described the 3D experience as "like being sucked into the screen"; another likened it to seeing the match from the vantage points only available to the managers in their dugouts. The 3D pilot scheme was run by Sky BSB.

Clean team

Liverpool players of the famous 1970s and 1980s sides had a number of washing rituals. Winger Ian Callaghan showered before every match, striker David Johnson always took a bath, while David Fairclough washed his hands four times before going on the field.

Bouncy performance

Mexican winger Cuauhtemoc Blanco coined a new technique for beating defenders. Twice in a 1998 World Cup match against South Korea he wedged the ball between his feet and jumped between defenders in what the media dubbed the "Blanco Bounce".

Womanly wiles break curfew

Curfew breaking is nothing new for footballers away from home and some of the methods of doing it can be ingenious. Among the most creative was Celtic winger Patsy Gallacher, who decided to sneak out for a drink from the team's hotel in Dunbar in 1926. Enlisting the help of a hotel chambermaid, he borrowed a dress from her in order to slip out. So good was his cross-dressing ploy that club manager Willie Maley actually held a door open for Patsy, thus inadvertently aiding him to make good his escape.

Merson confesses

England and Arsenal midfielder Paul Merson shocked football when he confessed in 1995 to a £150-a-day cocaine habit. He escaped formal FA punishment but went into rehab. He later confessed to alcohol and gambling addictions, as well.

Speed bonnie boat . . .

Scotland winger Jimmy "Jinky" Johnstone started a sea-rescue drama before a 1974 match with England. After a night out in the Ayrshire town of Largs, where Scotland's traditional training camp was placed, the little winger stood in a rowing boat in the early hours to belt out a patriotic version of "Bonnie Scotland". What he didn't know, but his watching team-mates could see, was that Johnstone was drifting away with the tide towards Ireland. A lifeguard was called and Johnstone was reunited with the team, which beat England 2–0 the following day.

Jailed for high-speed car chase

It was not something the burly midfielder did on the field too often, but Jan Molby showed a clean pair of heels in 1988 – and sparked a car chase with police right into prison. After a drinking session, the Dane was spotted by police in his high-powered car on the wrong side of the road in Liverpool and tried to pull him over. Molby thought he could lose the law and shot off.. The law won the chase and Molby was caught and jailed for three months.

You reap what you throw

Former Chelsea full back Paddy Mulligan lost the chance of a high-profile job in 1980 because of someone's very long memory. Mulligan was in a straight fight with Eoin Hand for the vacant post of Republic of Ireland coach but lost out to the Limerick City manager – by just one vote. It was later revealed that the one member of the Football Association of Ireland committee who voted against Mulligan harbored a grudge against him because he suspected the player had once thrown a bread roll at him on an away trip.

Football legend's dark past

There had been mutterings of dark deeds concerning Herbert Chapman before he found fame with Huddersfield Town and Arsenal in the 1920s and 1930s. The truth about Chapman's involvement in the demise of Leeds City in 1920 will never be fully known but it is alleged Chapman was a dab hand with matches. He was manager of City when it was expelled from the league for illegal payments to players and it has been alleged he took the club's books home and burned any evidence in his back garden.

Pirates of the Caribbean

A pirate league shook up the football world from 1949 to 1954. The so-called Colombia El Dorado for a while attracted some of the biggest stars of the era before it ended in recriminations over money. Colombia broke away from FIFA to set up a seemingly cash-rich professional division. Spanish ace Alfredo Di Stefano and England's Neil Franklin and Charlie Mitten were among the big-name signings promised fabulous signing-on fees. Many players were not paid and were almost held hostage by armed guards in their hotels. The disillusioned "mercenaries" left South America to not very warm welcomes back in their home countries.

Own-goal protest

The biggest recorded score in the world to date is 149–0 to Madagascan league champions AS Adema in 2002 – but they had some help. Opponents Stade Olympique L'Emryne scored 149 own goals in a bizarre protest over a previous refereeing decision.

Maldini's record medal haul

Italian legend Paolo Maldini has one of the largest collections of medals in football from 25 seasons at the top level. It includes three Champions League finals, three Intercontinental/World Club Cups, two Coppa Italias, three Supercoppas, a UEFA Super Cup final, a World Cup, a European Championship and three league titles. But it hasn't been success all the way for the classy defender who retired at 40 in 2009. He also has arguably the biggest number of runners-up medals – 17 – which includes a World Cup runner-up in 1994 and Euro 2000. Maldini, who played the whole of his club career with AC Milan, followed in his father Cesare's footsteps in winning the European Champions League.

Keeper-free zone

Colchester became the first English league club to have both goalkeepers dismissed in the same match. John Keeley and his understudy Nathan Munson were both sent off for professional fouls. Colchester lost 5–0 to Hereford.

Door Butcher-ed

Glasgow Rangers centre half Terry Butcher was fined £500 in 1988 by the Scottish FA for bringing the game into disrepute by kicking in the door of a referee's dressing room.

Unlucky break

Full back Celestine Babayaro broke his leg while celebrating a goal on his Chelsea debut during a pre-season game in 1997.

Ray pays in divorce ruling

Arsenal footballer Ray Parlour was ordered to pay his ex-wife Karen a third of his future earnings in a landmark 2004 divorce settlement. The couple, who had three children, had agreed a divorce settlement that awarded Karen two houses and a £250,000 lump sum but the maintenance was not agreed. A court awarded her £212,500 a year, but both parties were not satisfied and appealed. The UK Appeal Court increased Karen's award to £440,000 a year for five years to enable her to put aside £250,000 annually to build up her own capital.

Pasta to Italy

Paul Gascoigne, while homesick in Italy – the spiritual home of pasta – asked his family in England to send him a hamper of his favourite food. They sent packets of dried pasta.

Cambridge's moose myth explained

It has always been a source of confusion that Cambridge United from eastern England should be roared on by a moose mascot and moose impressions by supporters. Fan Dale Collett is credited with starting it in 1989. Arriving at the ground straight from a Spanish holiday without going home for a shower, Collett admitted the fact to his mates saying "Don't stand near me, I smell like a moose". They started bellowing moose calls and making antler impressions with their hands – something that went around the ground and stuck.

German corruption scandal

Hertha Berlin found themselves on the receiving end of competing bribes in a scandal that hit German football in 1971. Offenbacher Kickers offered the Berliners DM140,000 in return for a result that would send relegation rivals Arminia Bielefeld down. The dilemma for corrupt officials and players at Hertha was that they had already agreed a DM250,000 bribe from Arminia to throw the game in Arminia's favour. After Arminia's 1–0 win, Kickers' thwarted president Horst-Gregorio Canellas turned whistleblower. The subsequent German FA inquiry found 18 fixed matches and 52 players were banned. Canellas' life ban was later commuted to five years.

Higher priorities

Croatian Goran Granic revealed in 2009 why he was no longer tackling hard. The Hajduk Split defender's conversion to Catholicism is behind his softer style of play. He said: "God has created football for fun and relaxation. He would not like players to commit harsh fouls."

Fergie's retirement plan foiled

Former Everton striker Duncan Ferguson's 2001 attempt at making money through property development met with huge opposition from neighbours. Ferguson demolished a property he bought for £2m in the up-market Merseyside town of Formby and planned a development of 12 luxury flats that he could sell for £500,000 each, plus a detached luxury mansion. His plan was greeted with a storm of protests and petitions to the local council, which succeeded in getting the planning permission for the scheme rejected. Ferguson won on appeal but as of 2010 the plot lies empty with Ferguson living in Spain.

Ticket tout cons the FAI

The Republic of Ireland's qualification for the 1994 World Cup in the USA started a stampede for tickets – many thousands more than the Football Association of Ireland had been allocated. More than £210,000 was paid to a man who claimed to be a ticket agent and could satisfy the Irish appetite for only their second World Cup finals. But the man known only as "George the Greek" was a scamster and made off with the money without producing a single ticket. FAI honorary treasurer Joe Delaney shouldered the blame and paid the money back from his own pocket.

Mo crosses the divide

Mo Johnston became the first player to cross the sectarian divide between Glasgow Celtic and Rangers. In 1989 Catholic Johnston was the first high-profile member of his faith to join Protestant club Rangers.

Players fined for toilet-seat theft

Two highly paid English players were fined in 2007 for trying to steal a toilet seat from a DIY superstore. The incident involved Glen Johnson, reputed at the time to be on £30,000 a week with Chelsea, and Millwall striker Ben May. In what seemed an elaborate plot the duo tried to leave B&Q's Dartford store in Kent with the seat concealed in the packaging of a much cheaper type. The smirking pair were successfully "tackled" by a 74-year-old security guard and later fined £80 by magistrates for attempted theft.

Neville's eco-house plan

Manchester United full back Gary Neville revealed in 2010 that he is seeking permission to build an underground house below the moors of north-west England. Variously described in the media as a house fit for the Teletubbies or a James Bond movie villain, the £6–8m eco-friendly, subterranean mansion in the Bolton countryside would look flower-shaped from above with a huge kitchen forming a hub in the middle. Former England defender and Manchester United captain Neville wants the property to be powered by solar panels and a wind turbine. Planned facilities apart from dining rooms, bedrooms and bathrooms are a swimming pool, gym and office.

Cup of woes

One of the most disturbing exhibitions of violence in an English FA Cup final was in 1970 between arch-rivals Chelsea and Leeds United. Relentlessly brutal with a lot of hard men on the field at once, players were scythed down, headbutted and tackled high – without a single card being issued. Chelsea won 2–1.

Short stint

Jason Crowe's first-class debut for Arsenal lasted just 33 seconds. The 90th-minute substitute in a 1997 league cup tie was dismissed for a foul – at the time the fastest debut sending-off in English football history.

Gerrard cleared of affray charge

A row over the choice of music led Liverpool captain Steven Gerrard into the dock in 2009 to face a charge of affray. Gerrard was cleared but others in his group of friends pleaded guilty to their parts in a nightclub brawl. The fight started when Marcus McGhee was with a group that had been given control of the music selection for a party in the Merseyside bar. Gerrard approached McGhee looking to change the music, but McGhee took exception and refused to hand over control of the CD player. Words were exchanged and a fight involving others started. Gerrard admitted hitting McGhee but the jury accepted the England international's self-defence plea.

Directors rubbish their own fans

Newcastle directors Freddy Shepherd and Douglas Hall committed three cardinal sins – they rubbished not only their own club and star player, but also Geordie women. The pair were caught in a tabloid newspaper "sting" in 1998 in which they thought they were setting up a business deal with a wealthy Arab. During the recorded conversation in a Marbella brothel they mocked the club's own supporters for spending extortionate amounts of money on merchandise, called women supporters "dogs" and branded star striker Alan Shearer the "Mary Poppins of football".

Song of shame

Cameroon's Rigobert Song went home from the 1998 World Cup with an unwanted record – the first player to be dismissed from two World Cups. He was dismissed against Chile, having being sent off against Brazil in 1994. The 1994 dismissal also made him, at 17, the youngest to be sent off in the finals.

Mugger hits an own goal

A none-too-bright mugger was caught when he sat down to watch the Australia–Brazil game at the 2006 World Cup. He had found the ticket in a handbag he had snatched from Eva Standman in Munich – and decided to use it. The trouble was that the ticket was one of a pair and Eva's husband Berndt still went to the game. The mugger was rumbled as soon as he sat down beside Berndt. Vengeance was sweet as he called police who arrested the thief. Brazil won 2–0.

Forgetful Manny

A forgetful player cost his club a place in a lucrative cup competition in England. Manny Omoyinmi forgot he had played in the 1999–2000 league cup competition for another club so West Ham breached the rules when they played him following his transfer. With Manny, Hammers won, but football authorities ordered a replay, which they lost.

Striker's target was his team-mate

The beer – and blood – flowed when players from an English Premier League took an overseas weekend break in 1997. As revealed in a player's autobiography, things got nasty as a winger was knocked out in an alleged altercation with a striker who was also always on target for club and country. During one drinking session the winger had pushed his luck with the striker by flicking bottle tops at him and not heeding the warning signs. The pair went outside but only the striker returned upright. The winger, covered in blood, had to be carried in unconscious.

No Brits

Chelsea made English club history in 1999 by starting a league match against Southampton without a single British player in the side.

Dark goings on

Three floodlight failures in quick succession at English Premiership matches were believed to be sabotage in 1998. A Premier League inquiry suspected Far East gambling rings were trying to rig matches.

Doc's orders

Manchester United sacked their manager Tommy Docherty in 1977 for his love affair with the wife of club physiotherapist Laurie Brown. The club felt the affair had brought it into disrepute.

Peeing about?

Barry Fry, who managed nine English clubs including Birmingham and Peterborough, was advised that the best way to lift a gypsy curse and stop a run of bad luck was to urinate at each corner of the pitch. He said: "It's hard to squirt a bit out, walk 60 yards and do it again."

Flops made to stop

Following a disappointing 2010 World Cup first-round exit, Nigerian President Goodluck Jonathan threatened to not let the national team play another competitive match for two years. A spokesman claimed the move could 'help Nigeria reorganize its football.'

9/11 foursome fined for disrespect

A number of Chelsea players were fined by their club in 2001 for rowdy and drunken behaviour on the day of the World Trade Center disaster in New York. John Terry and team-mates Jody Morris, Frank Lampard and Eidur Gudjohnsen were drinking heavily at a Heathrow Airport hotel on the day of the 11 September attacks but the behavior was witnessed by many grieving Americans who were stranded by lack of flights home. There were also claims that there was some harassment of American tourists. The players went on their binge after a game against Levski Sofia had been called off – ironically out of respect for the victims of the terrorist attack.

Feeling sheepish after night out

Four unidentified players "kidnapped" a sheep while on a boozy night out in 2007. The names of the four have never been formally confirmed in connection with the sheep stealing but one was believed to have been a Welsh international and Premiership star. At 3am the four got a minibus home but stopped on the way and – for reasons best know to themselves – bundled a distressed sheep into the back and promptly forgot about it. Next morning they panicked at finding the sheep in the back garden, threw her in the back of the minibus and dropped her off in the first field they came to.

Jose misses out

Jose Mourinho missed the moment he won his first silverware with Chelsea in 2005. He was dismissed for putting his fingers to his lips in an apparent hush sign to opposition Liverpool fans, which the referee judged as inflammatory. He watched the celebrations on a stadium TV.

Football corruption 1906-style

The offering of "bungs" was not a phenomenon restricted to the late 20th- and early 21st-century football scenes – it also happened at the dawn of the game's popularity. The great Billy Meredith had been suspended for a year before he was transferred across town from Manchester City to rival United. Meredith was at the centre of a scandal that left City crippled because he was alleged to have offered a rival player a bribe to let City win and so advance their title chances. It failed, but an investigation led to an inspection of City's books for under-the-counter payments. Huge fines, players suspended and directors banned for life resulted.

Frau Schuster was the playmaker

Gaby Schuster didn't win any popularity contests as her husband Bernd's agent – and was accused of robbing Germany of one of its most gifted players. As coach Jupp Derwall's protégé midfielder, Schuster was propelled into the full German team at 20 and out of it by 23 as a result of Derwall's spat with Gaby. As Bernd's agent she negotiated his transfer from FC Koln to Barcelona and a furious Derwall told her: "You are a bad influence." Bernd, after 22 caps, never used his naturally gifted talents in the service of the national side again. Likened to Yoko Ono for her influence on her husband, she demanded DM1m for his return to the international scene, a sum which couldn't be raised even through sponsorship.

Lucky 13

Archie Thomson scored 13 goals for Australia as the Socceroos routed American Samoa 31–0 in a 2002 Oceania World Cup qualifying game.

Downfall of a founding father

Credited with being the founder of Association Football in Britain, the high-profile Preston North End chairman of the late 19th century, William Sudell, had a dark secret. He was a thief. Everything he achieved for Preston and the Football League of the time was based on fraud. His credits included the first treasurer of the Football League and making Preston such a great team that the "Invincibles" were unbeaten in 1888–89. On the debit side he was defrauding the cotton mill he managed of £6,000 over a number of years and funnelling the money to the football club where he had a reputation for lavish entertaining. In 1895 he was jailed and served three years.

Cup shame

Arsenal and Chelsea were fined a massive £100,000 each for some of the worst scenes of violence ever seen at a showpiece cup final. Twenty players were involved in a brawl towards the end of the 2007 league cup final, with players all over the pitch throwing punches.

Dave's rave

David Prutton of Southampton received a ten-match ban and a £6,000 fine in 2005 for refusing to walk when sent off and pushing referee Alan Wiley several times as he continued to argue.

Pierre's a striker – in many ways

Dutch forward Pierre Van Hooijdonk brought the mighty Nottingham Forest club to their knees in 1998 by going on strike. Newly promoted Forest reckoned they needed their big money stars to stay in the new English Premier League and rejected £4.5m Van Hooijdonk's transfer request because with 34 goals the previous season they viewed him as a great asset. Van Hooijdonk's reaction was to strike and he only returned with Forest in deep relegation trouble and too late for even his prolific goalscoring record to save. Forest went down and Van Hooijdonk was sold. Later he came back to haunt Forest with a claim for a loyalty bonus and got £383,000 in an out-of-court settlement.

"Token" woman row

Luton Town manager Mike Newell lashed out at having a woman linesman – especially as Ann Raynor did not award the penalty he thought his side should have. Newell ranted: "She shouldn't be here. It is tokenism for politically correct idiots." He was fined £6,500 by the FA.

29 spectators turn up for cup tie

Players were close to outnumbering the crowd when ailing Scottish club Clydebank played East Stirling in a league cup tie in 1999. The teams played before a crowd of 29, at the time the lowest British attendance record. Clydebank was a club in crisis with foreign owners, having to play their home matches at Greenock and a disgruntled fan base. The lack of spectators was exacerbated by it being a hot day during the July holiday season and there being a major sailing event at nearby Greenock. Clydebank played out a 2–1 defeat in an almost eerie silence in a match even their own directors didn't turn up for.

Feathers fly over Tevez chicken taunt

Things got in a flap when Carlos Tevez flapped his arms like a chicken in celebration of a goal in 2004. The Boca Juniors' striker could not have been more inflammatory because the opposition River Plate had been dubbed "hens" some years before for several times snatching defeat from the jaws of victory. Tevez, later to join Manchester United in controversial circumstances, was sent off for inflaming the River Plate fans and in explaining why he was red-carding him, the ref seemed to make things worse by flapping his own arms on three occasions.

Footballer's early mid-life crisis?

At the age of 34 Germany goalkeeper Oliver Kahn went all trendy with different clothes and a sudden appreciation for techno music. The reason for the Bayern Munich custodian's changes was his high-profile relationship with a barmaid 13 years his junior, which hit the German media in 2003. His response to questions about why he walked out on his eight-months-pregnant wife Simone for the 21-year-old was: "I am not the Pope." Encouraged by his young new love, Kahn was seen in trendy nightclubs in clothes deemed, by the media especially, inappropriate for his age.

Keegan confesses England failings

Kevin Keegan made a refreshingly frank public confession of failure when he suddenly quit as England's national coach in 2000. After a successful career as a player, Keegan was a nearly man at managerial level. He won nothing as a club manager or at national level. His crisis of confidence came after a poor and uninspired England performance saw them beaten 1–0 by Germany at Wembley. With the players barely off the field, volatile Keegan was quitting saying he "couldn't find that little bit extra".

Freddie's pants ad cut down to size

Massive posters of Freddie Ljungberg stripped down to skimpy underpants were seen the world over from 2002 after the Swede signed a modelling contract with Calvin Klein. Dubbed the "sexy Swedish stallion" by adoring women among his fans, it cut no ice with Ljungberg's Arsenal or international team-mates in the harsh mickey-taking environment of the dressing room. Ljungberg had not anticipated the fuss and became embarrassed by his modelling work. He resorted to bribing his team-mates with free underwear, as modelled by him, to shut them up.

Exeter exit had Geller in charge

A small West Country English club had an extraordinary board make-up in 2002 – cabaret artist Uri Geller as joint chairman and his friend Michael Jackson as a director. High-powered stuff, with a man who can bend spoons with his mind and one of the superstars of pop on board, but their success was not to rub off on Exeter City that season. Geller agreed to play fair with Exeter's opponents by not trying any paranormal activity and within a year the club was in the dumps and out of the Football League for the first time in over 80 years.

Barely possible

India withdrew from the 1950 World Cup finals because the team was not used to playing in boots and FIFA refused to let their team play barefoot. India has never come near to qualifying since.

Ref gets an ass kicking

1920's Newcastle star Hughie Gallacher was a no-nonsense player and one to take his chances off the field as well as on. After a run-in with a referee that led to a booking in a 1927 league match, the 5-foot 5-inch winger kicked the ref into a bath, neat footwork that cost him a two-month suspension. During the booking altercation, Gallacher had demanded the ref's name. On being told "Fogg", Gallacher retorted: "You've been in one all afternoon." Gallacher had actually gone to the referee's dressing room to apologise but when he saw the official bending over the bath, revenge took precedence.

Star Lawton relegates himself

At the peak of his powers in 1947 England golden boy Tommy Lawton deliberately moved to a club two divisions lower in the English league. Fans were aghast on two fronts: that prolific centre forward Lawton should move to unfashionable Third Division club Notts County and that County could afford the £20,000 record transfer fee required. Lawton had played at the top level for years with Everton and Chelsea, and in 151 subsequent appearances for County he scored 90 goals, which in the 1949–50 season helped them to promotion. The bizarre move down the leagues has never been fully explained but a factor may have Lawton's friendship with former Chelsea physiotherapist Arthur Stollery, who was managing County at the time.

French farce

Former French national coach Jacques Santini lasted just 13 games as manager of Tottenham Hotspur before disappointing results saw him replaced.

Ten-minute job

Leroy Rosenior created a record by holding a manager's job – for just ten minutes. He was reappointed to Torquay United just as they were relegated from the English football league, but minutes later the club was sold and the new owners wanted their own man.

Bogus buyer has Carlisle in a spin

A potential investor bid £6m for a stake in Carlisle United in 2001 but far from being the millionaire he claimed to be, he was revealed as a curry restaurant waiter. The Walter Mitty character carried on the fantasy for weeks claiming he could afford the millions for a 25 per cent stake in England's most northerly league club. He even attended a press conference and smoothly outlined his plans to invest in Carlisle after the sale of a Spanish hotel went through. He failed to come up with the money on deadline and the truth began to filter out after the club lost patience with him.

S**t ref?

The referee accused of ending Italy's 2002 World Cup dream has a toilet block named after him. Ecuadorian Byron Moreno's name is on public loos at Sicily's Santa Teresa Riva resort after he disallowed a golden goal, turned down a penalty claim and sent off Francesco Totti. Italy lost 2–1 to South Korea.

Smuggling goalkeeper lands in jail

Ricardo Zamora, one of Spain's greatest ever goalkeepers, could smuggle the ball off the toe of advancing forwards but not cigars. On his way back from Belgium where he was sent home from the Antwerp Olympic Games in 1920 for punching an opponent, Spanish border guards arrested him for smuggling Havana cigars. The man adoring fans called "El Divino", the Divine One, found himself behind bars for a while and then fined. His brilliant performances on the pitch came despite his love of cigars, cognac and a reputed 60 cigarettes a day.

Zagreb's Zdravko shakes them up

Zdravko Mamic is undoubtedly one of the more colourful characters to come out of Croatian football. The vice-president of Dinamo Zagreb between 2003 and 2009 hasn't held back his opinion and police, Croatian FA officials, town planners and journalists have all felt the full force of his temper.

Barca donate shirt sponsorship

One of potentially the most lucrative and successful spaces for shirt sponsorship has never been made available to commercial companies. It is a boast of Spanish league giants and 2009 European Champions Barcelona that in 107 years the famous blue and red striped shirts have been logo-free and offers of over £25m have been turned down. That came to an end in 2006 when logos for the United Nations Children's Fund (Unicef) were allowed and have appeared on the shirts of such Barca superstars as Lionel Messi and Thierry Henry – for free. President Joan Laporta said: "We are very proud to donate our shirt to the children of the world."

Football's answer to recession blues

Spanish league club Villarreal acted to make sure that the 2008–09 recession didn't rob fans of their football therapy. Club president Fernando Roig promised free tickets for the 2009–10 season for supporters who lost their jobs in the economic crisis. Club employees, including players and sponsors, contributed to a fund set up to provide free seats at the Madrigal Stadium. Roig said: "We were thinking of the wide social base the club has and making sure those who have lost their jobs continue to watch us."

Clough cuffs them

Nottingham Forest manager Brian Clough's crusade against unruly fans came to a head in 1989 when millions of TV viewers watched him grab and punch fans who were invading the pitch at the end of a 5–2 cup win.

Niall's pockets are deep

Irish international turned Sunderland chairman Niall Quinn bailed out 80 club fans who had been grounded by an airline for singing on an aircraft. The rousing songs were not appreciated at Bristol Airport and they were thrown off more than 300 miles from home. Quinn, of whom they had been singing, organised a fleet of 18 taxis to get the loyal bunch back home to Wearside. He footed the bill, which came to £8,000. Quinn had years before donated the whole £1m proceeds of his testimonial night to a children's hospital.

What they really say on the field

TV viewers in Britain got a taste – or rather an earful – of what is really said in the heat of battle on a football field. Referee David Elleray was secretly miked up for a 2000 TV progamme called *Out of Order* and none of the players in the Millwall–Arsenal London derby knew. It meant they didn't hold back on their language and much of it had to be bleeped out to save viewers' blushes. Typical of the dialogue was when Elleray disallowed a Tony Adams "goal". The big Arsenal centre half called the ref a "f***ing cheat" and earned himself an immediate booking.

No tender, loving care

An international defender who revelled in his hard-man image for injuring opponents, cultivated this image with some aplomb and cleverness. But scything tackles were not the only weapon in his armoury when man-marking. In one match he sidled up to an opposing forward and stuck a finger up his victim's rectum – with the obvious disabling and disconcerting effect. But the defender's secret was that he was a trained doctor so he knew what he was doing with this free on-field prostate examination.

Contract negotiations – with a gun!

Aston Villa villain defender Frank Barson knew a thing or two about violence. He was friends with a pair of brothers who were hanged for murder and was reputed to have taken a gun into negotiations about pay – no doubt to focus the manager's mind. He was the archetypal hard man of the era either side of World War 1; one tackle on a Fulham opponent in the 1920s was deemed so out of order it earned Barson a seven-month ban. Once, when playing for Barnsley, he had to be smuggled out of Everton's ground because a furious mob of home fans was waiting for him.

No change is a surprise

Squad-rotation specialist Rafa Benitez went for 100 games until 2007 before he put out the same Liverpool starting line-up two games running.

Unwanted record

Derby County suffered the earliest English Premier League relegation ever in 2008. The team was doomed by their 32nd fixture with the lowest number of points (11), one win and the largest goal difference of -69.

Chat injury

Manchester United keeper Alex Stepney dislocated his jaw while shouting at his defenders during a game against Birmingham City in 1975.

World Cup group of certain death

Scotland players found themselves kicked, quite literally, out of the 1986 World Cup in one of the most disgraceful games ever seen at the prestigious finals. Uruguay needed to beat Scotland to ensure going through to the knockout phase and were prepared to kick their way through. Jose Batista set the tone for the game with the quickest sending off in World Cup finals' history – 56 seconds – for a tackle on Gordon Strachan. The Uruguayans kicked the Scottish team to pieces for the next 90 minutes in a widely condemned and cynical display. Scotland, bottom of their group after the 0–0 draw, had the satisfaction of not caving in to give Uruguay the win they needed to progress.

Changing sides

A 1970s hard man was reported to have changed sides and is living as a woman in San Francisco. Club officials discovered the player's "sexual transfer" when they invited him to the club's centenary celebrations.

Team-mates on a collision course

Graeme Le Saux broke his hand – punching a Blackburn Rovers team-mate for encroaching on his territory. Tension was already high in the Blackburn side because their winning touch had deserted them since taking the English Premier League title in 1994 and reached boiling point in a 3–0 Champions League defeat by Spartak Moscow. Wing back Le Saux had been known to complain that midfielder David Batty retreated too far on to his flank and seemed to be proved right when the two collided. Despite being on the same side they clashed violently – an incident seen by millions on TV.

Batted – by a tricycle

A crashing tackle from behind gave Leeds United midfield hardman David Batty a taste of his own medicine in 1998. His son crashed into him at high speed on a tricycle, damaging Batty's achilles tendon and sidelining him for several weeks.

Knife-edge decision

Goalkeeper Chris Woods slashed his finger on a penknife while cutting the string of his tracksuit bottoms. He had to pull out of an England international, allowing David Seaman to take over.

Smells funny

Spain's Santiago Canizares was ruled out of the 2002 World Cup after dropping a bottle of aftershave and severing tendons in his foot.

Dean's mistaken identity crisis

"Revenge is a dish best eaten cold" might have been the mantra for goal machine of the 1920s and 1930s Dixie Dean. The man who hit 43 hat-tricks in his career was both fiery and had what he thought was a good memory. He couldn't forget the man whose crunching tackle meant Dean lost a testicle at 17. Dean, an Everton favourite, believed his assailant was an Altrincham player called Parks and when he saw him 17 years later in a Liverpool pub Dean floored him even though Parks had treated him to a pint of beer. It was only established some time later that Dean's injury had been inflicted by a player called Molyneux.

Shot hits the fan

A furious goalkeeper injured two spectators when he lashed the ball into the crowd. Police were called in after Notts County keeper Stuart Nelson vented his anger at going 2-0 down to Hartlepool United by angrily booting the ball into the crowd, injuring one person on the arm and another on the head. Nelson's temper would not improve as County eventually lost the 2012 League One match 3-0.

Coach's revenge – a 10-mile walk

Romanian league goalkeeper Bogdan Vintila will always remember the 1999 soft goal he let in. He hasn't remembered it for the actual incident in which Universitatea Craiova scored aginst Vintila's team Arges Pitesti but for the consequences that followed. Arges Pitesti's coach Florin Halagian was known as a disciplinarian and was furious with his keeper's slack performance. In order to get him focused for future games Halagian stopped the team bus as it passed through a forest and threw the goalkeeper off. Vintila had to walk 10 miles through rough woodland before he found a lift home.

Scooter burn-up plot flops

Weapons for fans intent on football mayhem have come in various forms over the years but there are none stranger than a burning scooter. The blazing vehicle was an unwanted present from Internazionale's notorious Ultras in 2001. Intent on trouble with Atalanta visiting the San Siro stadium in Milan, the Ultras relieved a visitor of his scooter and, in an amazing lapse of security, managed to smuggle it into the stadium in Milan. They set it on fire and threw it from an upper tier only for it fortunately to land on a section of empty terracing below.

Training to lie

Momo Sissoko thought he had the perfect excuse for missing a couple of Valencia training sessions in 2004. He claimed he was playing for Mali against Kenya, a match that never took place. He even made up a bogus result of Mali 0, Kenya 1.

Keane–Haaland grudge match

One of the football episodes involving uncompromising hatred had two distinct parts – four years apart. Part one was in 1997 when Manchester United's Roy Keane fouled Alf-Inge Haaland of Leeds United but also injured himself in the process. All Keane heard through his agony was Haaland saying, "Stop faking it." Part two took place in 2001 when Haaland was playing for Manchester City – Keane flew in with a revenge tackle aimed at Haaland's knee rather than the ball. Keane was right on target and stood over his victim, returning the taunts. Norwegian international Haaland never played a full match again and retired. Keane was only fined by the FA.

Burning ambition

Andy Dibble suffered burns from the chemicals in the white lines of the pitch as he kept goal for Barry Town against Carmarthen Town.

Maradona butchered by hard man

Andoni Goikoetxea will go down in football history as the man who nailed the big prize – Diego Maradona. The 6-foot 1-inch Atletico Bilbao defender revelled in the title of "the Butcher of Bilbao" for the ferocious tackle from behind in 1983 that severely injured 5-foot 5-inch Maradona's ankle – an injury that came close to putting the Argentinian out of the game.

No fooling around in Jamaica riot

April Fool's Day was significant with what was to transpire when the Jamaican national team arranged a friendly with local side Toros Neza in 1997. The word friendly went out the window on 19 minutes when a Toros victim of a bad tackle responded with a punch in the face for his aggressor. Both teams got involved in punching and kicking for more than five minutes before the Jamaica side walked off. Those who thought it was all over were wrong because they came back with bricks, broken bottles and a chair with which to carry on the fight. Needless to say the match was abandoned, but Jamaica qualified for the 1998 World Cup finals.

Bottled out

A dodgy bottle of lager proved fatal to England's World Cup quarter-final against West Germany in 1970. Goalkeeper Gordon Banks was taken ill after drinking the beer; Peter Bonetti replaced him and his errors led to a German comeback to win 3–2.

Wrong box

Former Manchester United goalkeeper Peter Schmeichel pulled a hamstring while attempting to tackle Arsenal's Dennis Bergkamp. Ironically, the tackle took place on the edge of Arsenal's 18-yard box and 80 yards from Peter's own goal.

Tears for fear

Italian police managed to KO England goalkeeper Ray Clemence with tear gas during the opening game of the 1980 European Championships. They released the gas after trouble broke out on the terraces behind Clemence's goal, but the keeper was also overcome.

Muscat finds global hatred

Australian hard-as-nails defender Kevin Muscat was once described as the most hated man in football for his uncompromising approach and crunching tackles. His charge sheet includes being successfully sued by Matt Holmes of Charlton for a career-ending challenge that broke his leg and led to an award of £250,000. Muscat also dished out serious injuries to Welsh international Craig Bellamy, and a challenge on France's Christophe Dugarry was described by French coach Roger Lemerre as "an act of brutality".

Windass wind-up

Striker Dean Windass was out of favour as a first choice for Hull City but as a substitute he was given a strange role in a 2008 Premiership match against Stoke City. City's Rory Delap had a devastating, long throw-in technique and Windass was told to distract him by warming up near him. Windass' theatrical antics attracted the ref's attention, who booked him for "ungentlemanly conduct".

Bent rage

England striker Darren Bent was livid when his Tottenham Hotspur manager Harry Redknapp quipped over Bent missing a sitter in a match: "My wife could have put that one away." Sandra Redknapp's relationship with Harry was more durable than Bent's, who was sold to Sunderland months later in 2009.

What an arse

Wales and Middlesbrough goalkeeper Mark Crossley ended up in bed for seven weeks after landing on his backside while taking a goal kick during a pre-season friendly in Finland in 1997.

Fishy business

A dodgy pre-match meal of plaice in 1902 was blamed on Stoke City having only seven fit players left by half-time. Goalkeeper Leigh Richmond Roose was first to be laid low by the food poisoning and lasted just ten minutes of the league game against Liverpool.

Winners lose all

Russians who refused even to bow to their Nazi captors on the football field paid for victory with their lives in 1942. The Start team from Kiev was ordered to play a Luftwaffe side and because they contained several pre-war Dinamo Kiev stars, they won. It has been never clear if the Start team realised that they were required to "throw" a match to the Germans, but when a rematch was ordered they went out – and won again. Nazi pride dented, retribution was swift and the Start team was arrested. One, alleged to have been an intelligence officer, died under torture, while three more of the team were shot in a prison camp.

Cup match proved fatal

One person dead, another with a fractured skull and many others injured sounds like the aftermath of a train crash. No, it was a 1971 Copa Libertadores match between Argentina's Boca Juniors and Sporting Cristal of Peru. A dive in the penalty box by Boca's Robert Rogel started a mass brawl in which only Sporting's goalkeeper was not red-carded, but his skipper Fernando Mellan suffered brain damage from a skull fracture. The whole debacle was televised and the mother of Sporting's Orlando de la Torre died of a heart attack as she watched. Various grades of assault charges followed, including grievous bodily harm, and some players were imprisoned.

Schumacher savages Battiston

France's President Mitterand and German Chancellor Helmut Kohl had to step in to quieten public feelings after a 1982 World Cup incident. They issued a joint plea for calm after German goalkeeper Harald Schumacher's savage elbow attack on France's Patrick Battiston in a thrilling semi-final. A World Cup final place rested on the outcome of Battiston's one on one with Schumacher. As Battiston released his shot Schumacher kept on coming with his elbow and took out the player – and two of his teeth, which led to the Frenchman being stretchered off with a suspected broken neck. After a 3–3 draw Germany won on penalties, but the furore was made worse by Schumacher's cynical offer to pay for Battiston's new teeth.

Bulgarian derby gets out of hand

Local derbies are always fraught with tension and partisanship and none proved it more than the Bulgarian Cup final of 1985 between two clubs from the capital Sofia, CSKA and Levski. On the field it was a matter of tempers flaring, sparked by dubious penalties and a handled goal. The ref was attacked twice and two players sent off. After the final whistle a mass brawl started off the field and had to be broken up by police. The Bulgarian FA, appalled at the shameful scenes, initially dissolved both clubs and gave five players life bans but eased the sanctions at a later review.

Coke smuggler

An Israeli player was jailed for four and a half years for smuggling 5 kilos of cocaine into the country in 2003. The defender denied the allegations but served around two years.

Souness comeback is an inspiration

If ever a side had all the inspiration it needed to win England's FA Cup it was Liverpool of 1992. Their manager Graeme Souness climbed from his hospital bed while recovering from heart bypass surgery to manage them on Cup Final day against Sunderland. With a doctor sitting beside him, Souness, a hard but inspirational figure as a midfielder in his playing days, was a shining example to his team. Looking drawn and ill he gave his side their game plan and he watched as they won 2–0. Souness' grit and subsequent recovery were remarkable in that it had only been a few weeks before at the cup semi-final stage that he told his players of his need for a triple heart bypass.

Bottled out

A Dunfermline Athletic goalkeeper by the name of Slavin was stretchered off the pitch during a match in 1911, apparently drunk.

How Stalin treated Soviet failure

Soviet dictator Joseph Stalin did not take failure or slights to Russian pride lightly. When that happened his vengeance was swift and hard and it led to a Moscow football club being disbanded in 1952 and three players banned for life. Soviet state prestige took a dive in an Olympic Games tie between the Soviets, made up mainly of CDSA Moscow personnel, and Yugoslavia, which had recently broken away from Russian influence. After a 5–5 draw, Yugoslavia won 3–1, leaving Stalin furious. On his orders CDSA Moscow was no more and three players – Konstantin Kryzhevsky, Anatoly Bashashkin and Konstantin Beskow – were banned for the game for life. Fortunately for them all, Stalin died within a year and their sentences were commuted.

Door catch

Mark Statham of English non-league club Stalybridge Celtic missed a game in 1999 after getting his head trapped in a car door.

Making a meal of it

German international Norbert Nigbur's football career was all but finished getting up to leave a restaurant table in 1980. He tore the meniscus cartilage in his knee, locking it in the process.

Lofty perch

Everton goalkeeper Richard Wright missed the start of the 2003–04 season after falling out of his loft and injuring his shoulder.

Thanks, mate

Millwall's Bryan King was felled by a practical joke that went wrong. Team "mate" Billy Neil was meant to pull his punch in a pre-match prank but ended up whacking his goalkeeper in the eye with his sovereign ring. The wound required six stitches.

Creamed

Former Wimbledon and Nottingham Forest keeper Dave Beasant had to pull out of a game after dropping a salad cream bottle on his foot while making a sandwich.

Giants falter in FA Cup final

Underdogs Wimbledon waited for the greatest stage of all – a Wembley final – before engineering one of the greatest English FA Cup upsets of all time. Wimbledon, a collection of renowned jokers who 10 years before had been playing non-league games in front of crowds totalling just hundreds, beat an expensively put together Liverpool to win the 1988 FA Cup. The decisive goal in the 1–0 victory was by Lawrie Sanchez and Liverpool, looking for their second league and cup double, couldn't break Wimbledon's stranglehold. To cap it all a penalty was saved in the final for the first time when Dons' Dave Beasant parried John Aldridge's shot.

Arsenal–United tension boils over

The English FA was sufficiently ashamed of the behaviour of Arsenal and Manchester United players in 1990 that they docked points from both clubs. Events after an innocuous tackle by Gunners full back Nigel Winterburn flared out of control with a 21-man fracas on the pitch with kicks, punching and chest shoving. Arsenal's Anders Limpar ended up pushed over an advertising hoarding. Arsenal were docked two points and United one, but the brawl didn't stop Arsenal winning 1–0 on the day and the League Championship at the end of the season To this day Gunners–United games remain hair-trigger affairs.

Eggs-act shot

Grimsby goalkeeper Aidan Davison was felled by a hard-boiled egg during a Second Division play-off game against Fulham in 1998.

Professional foul is outlawed

The enduring act of cynicism in a showpiece FA Cup final in 1980 led to a change in football law. Teenager Paul Allen of West Ham was speeding into football history when he bore down on Arsenal's goal in a one-to-one with keeper Pat Jennings. Scoring would make Allen – at 17 years and 256 days old – the youngest goalscorer in a Wembley final, but the pursuing Arsenal centre half Willie Young had other ideas. With the classic stop-him-at-all-costs "professional foul" he cynically tripped Allen from behind to rob him of his glory. The incident led to an outcry and the professional foul was outlawed soon after. Allen had the last laugh, though, as the youngest FA Cup medal winner when West Ham won 1–0.

Pundit Savage gets his comeuppance

"Savage by name – savage by nature" had often been levelled at Welshman Robbie Savage. His strong-arm midfield style made few friends in the early 21st-century English game for Leicester City and Derby County. Retribution came unexpectedly, and literally, out of the blue when he was smashed in the face while seated in a radio commentary box in 2010 where he was working for the BBC as a summariser. Aston Villa captain Stiliyan Petrov had hiked the ball into the stand and left the Welshman with a bloody nose, which prompted cheers from amused crowd of spectators seated around him. Despite the pain, Savage laughed off the incident and carried on.

Remote chance

Arsenal's custodian David Seaman missed the first half of the 1996–97 season after damaging his knee ligaments bending down for the TV remote control box.

Two-minute United career for keeper

No one could have accused Nick Culkin of lacking patience but it was not to be rewarded. His first team playing career for Manchester United lasted just two minutes in 1999. After being signed as a 16-year-old goalkeeper he spent four years working his way to the top squad before making a single, short-lived, first team appearance. Coming on as the 89th-minute replacement for Raimond Van der Gouw, Culkin took a goal kick before, two minutes later, the final whistle blew. He never played for United's first team again but played for other clubs before succumbing to injury in 2005.

Jermaine Pennant, man of letters

Former football girlfriend Amii Groves revealed the secret of her life with Liverpool winger Jermaine Pennant in 2008 – Scrabble. Dogged by off-the-field problems early in his career, Pennant was encouraged to take up board games such as Scrabble. She was quoted as saying that Pennant became hooked on the word game and spent ages saving up the letters to make up "zoo", which he thought was a high score. Amii said they split two months after getting engaged – in a row sparked by Scrabble.

Kick-out blackout

Portsmouth goalkeeper Aaron Flahavan fainted as he took a goal kick during a league cup tie against Blackburn Rovers. It was the second time it had happened and high blood pressure was blamed.

Injury jinx halts Bulgarian game

An injury plague and suspensions left Bulgarian third division side Gigant Belene with a tough task in their 2009 match with Chavdar Byala. Gigant took the field with just the eight players that they had left in their squad and the referee Stoyan Denev allowed it to go ahead. With no substitutes it was inevitable that injuries would be befall the depleted Gigant and it happened not once, but twice. With Gigant down to six players the referee applied the league rules and abandoned the match. Chavdar Byala was awarded a 3–0 win.

Iron man

Liverpool reserve goalkeeper Michael Stensgaard's Anfield career was brought to an untimely end when he dislocated his shoulder while erecting an ironing board.

In a spin

Agile Celtic winger Patsy Gallacher scored the winning goal in the 1925 Scottish Cup final by jamming the ball between his feet in a crowded penalty area and somersaulting himself into the net.

Hand handicap

Hungarian international keeper Karoly Zsak won 30 caps for his country until 1925 despite having had a finger amputated.

World Record with his head

Martin Palermo reckons he headed himself straight into the *Guinness World Records* in 2009 with a world record goal. He nodded home from 38.9 metres for Boca Juniors in an Argentinian league match win over Velez Sarsfield. It was a vital goal in Boca's 3–2 win and it came from the halfway line. Palermo was in the centre circle when Velez goalkeeper German Montoya booted the ball clear and it came to Palermo at just over head height. Palermo powered it straight back into the net. Palermo has applied for a *Guinness World Record* after searching for, but not finding, similar incidents.

Sight problem

Scottish goalkeeper Jim Leighton had to be substituted after losing a contact lens during a match.

Ahn's glory goal becomes own goal

South Korean star Ahn Jung-Hwan was sacked by his club for scoring a World Cup goal in 2002. His effort knocked Italy out of the competition but Ahn's problem was that he played on loan for Italian Serie A side Perugia. Furious Perugia president Luciano Gaucci told the South Korean not to return to the club, saying: "That gentleman will never set foot in Perugia again. I'm a nationalist and regard such behaviour not only as an affront to Italian pride. I have no intention of paying a salary to someone who has ruined Italian football." Perugia later retracted the comments and offered to buy Ahn's contract, but the player was sufficiently upset to refuse to join them.

Caught up

Queen's Park goalkeeper Andrew Baird got his hand caught in the net during an 1894 Scottish Cup tie and could only watch as Rangers centre forward David Boyd scored.

Rocky horror

Zimbabwe goalkeeper Bruce Grobbelaar needed a brain scan in 1993 after being hit on the head with a rock during a World Cup qualifying match against Egypt.

Owner's crimes against football

It must have been a strange sight to see Red Star Belgrade's players stripping off and changing in the car park of city rivals Obilic's ground but this was a team taking no chances. From 1998 Obilic was owned by Zeljko Raznatovic, better known as Serbian paramilitary leader, Arkan. He had promised Obilic's success-starved fans the Yugoslav title – and delivered. How it was done is what was controversial. There were allegations of intimidation, with opposition players suddenly withdrawing from games, and that sedative gases were pumped into opposition dressing rooms – hence the car park changing rooms. Indicted by the UN for crimes against humanity, Arkan was assassinated in 2000.

Smashing time

Paul Gascoigne reacted badly when told he was being dropped from England's 1998 World Cup squad. The midfielder, who had previously attracted more bad press from excessive drinking, was reported to have smashed up England coach Glenn Hoddle's hotel room.

Commentator hadn't the foggiest

The 1940 Hibernian–Hearts Edinburgh derby was not an easy assignment for BBC football commentator Bob Kingsley. First of all it was wartime Britain and Kingsley was not allowed to mention the weather in case German pilots were listening. But the conditions could not have been worse for an air raid as it was thick fog and Kingsley could not mention that either. Unable to see the game, he let his imagination run riot and described a sunny game with plenty of goals. Although he couldn't see the game, what was really going on behind the blanket of fog was even more fantastic with a 6–5 Hearts win. Spectators didn't know the score or that the match had finished until the fog lifted.

Rough justice

Vietnamese keeper Do Ngoc The was stabbed outside a nightclub by a disgruntled opposition fan. Playing for Danang, he had kept a clean sheet in a V-League game and his side had caused an upset by beating Song Lam Nghe 1–0.

Belly secret

Charlton Athletic goalkeeper Sam Bartram had a hot poultice on his stomach to counter the effects of food poisoning while playing Newcastle United in the 1947 FA Cup semi-final. Charlton won and went on to win the cup final.

River catch

For years Notts County in England employed coracle maker Fred Davies to station himself on the local river during matches to retrieve balls that had flown out from their Gay Meadow ground.

Tony Blair's memory problem

The historians and statisticians among Newcastle United's fanatical supporters went into overdrive to dispute British Prime Minister Tony Blair's claimed long-time allegiance to the club. After coming to power in 1997 Blair said in an interview he remembered sitting in the St James' Park Gallowgate End and watching legendary striker Jackie Milburn. With the "allegiance" seen as a ploy to secure the Geordie working-class vote, Blair's assertions were quickly proved wrong as Blair was only four when Milburn retired and the installation of seating in the Gallowgate End was four decades away.

Careless hands

Every keeper nightmare happened to Leeds United's goalkeeper Gary Sprake in 1967. In front of Liverpool's notoriously vocal Kop he aborted a throw out and spooned the ball over his shoulder for an own goal.

Clucking nuisance

Brazilian World Cup star Romario was ordered to pay damages for attacking a fan who threw chickens at him during a 2003 training-ground fracas. The feathers – and fists – flew when the fan protested against Fluminense's terrible form.

Wolves roar

A TV April Fool's Day story in 1994 caused uproar at Wolverhampton Wanderers. The club's switchboard was flooded with calls from angry fans after the story claimed the-then manager Graham Taylor was changing the club's strip to white from the traditional gold.

Hosepipe ploy déjà vu

The astute eye of Wolverhampton Wanderers manager Stan Cullis spotted a chink in the armour of the great Hungarian players of the early 1950s. Cullis had noted in the 1954 World Cup final in Switzerland that Hungary had faded badly on a quagmire of a pitch at the Wankdorf Stadium in Berne and lost a two-goal lead to be defeated 3–2 by West Germany. Cullis remembered this for a home friendly with Honved, which comprised many of Hungary's international players, and ordered three apprentices on to the muddy Molyneux pitch with hosepipes to soak it even more. True to form, Honved squandered a two-goal lead to lose 3–2 again.

Flare up

A Milan derby match in 2005 was abandoned when AC's Brazilian goalkeeper Dida was hit and injured by a flare thrown from the crowd.

Name changes fail to change luck

London club Leyton Orient has had more name changes than most and has never found one that brought them success in the English league or FA Cup. Formed by members of the Glyn Cricket Club in 1881, it became Eagle Cricket Club in 1886, then Orient Football Club, after the locally based Orient Shipping Company, in 1888. Reflecting the more gentrified area in which it played, it became Clapton Orient by 1898. By 1956 it was Leyton Orient and 1966 just Orient. Fan pressure in 1987 forced the resumption of the Leyton Orient label.

Laid out

Celtic's Ronnie Simpson was struck on the head by a brick while warming up for a World Club Cup match against Racing Club of Argentina in 1967. He was unable to play and reserve John Fallon replaced him.

Murder bid charge

A firework-throwing fan was arrested and charged with attempted murder in 1987 after Cyprus goalkeeper Andreas Charitou suffered a heart attack as a result.

Triumph and tragedy

Steaua Bucharest goalkeeper Helmuth Duckadam's career came to a premature end with a rare blood disorder soon after he saved four consecutive penalties in the 1986 European Cup final penalty shoot-out win over Barcelona.

Ring injury

Argentine goalkeeper Nery Pumpido almost lost a finger in a freak training-ground accident when he caught his wedding ring on a nail on the crossbar.

Pet hate

Kaizer Chiefs and South Africa goalkeeper Rowen Fernandez had to be hospitalised after being bitten by a pet spider.

Spanish Civil War lingers on

It may have ended in 1939 but the remnants of the Spanish Civil War live on between Barcelona and Real Madrid. Meetings to this day are feisty between Real, forever associated with dictator General Franco, and Barca with its fiercely Catalan and Republican support, but one of the most bizarre meetings was in 1943. Barca had won the first leg of a Copa del Rey semi-final 3–0 and Real needed a masterstroke to turn things around. It came in the form of the Franco regime's director of state security visiting the Barcelona dressing room – with a gun in his hand. Small wonder Real hauled back the first-leg deficit, and what's more, with an 11–1 win.

Diving keeper

Real Madrid goalkeeper Paco Buyo was suspended in 1988 – for diving. Atletico Madrid's Paolo Futre was sent off for "punching" Buyo, but TV replays showed Buyo had fallen without being hit.

Shy slaphead

Irish international Tommy Priestley, who played for Chelsea in the 1930s, wore a Petr Cech-style skull cap – because he was self-conscious about his baldness.

Ticket trouble

TV pundit Robbie Earle's lucrative television contract was terminated when his ticket allocation for a 2010 World Cup game were used for an illegal ambush marketing campaign. A Dutch beer company, who were not one of the tournament's official sponsors, attempted to gain exposure by distributing the tickets to 36 women clad in mini-dresses.

Self-harming keeper swings the match

Esperance goalkeeper Chokri El Ouaer thought he had the necessary game-turning ploy needed when his Tunisian side faced defeat in the 2000 African Champions League final with minutes to go. Behind on away goals, El Ouaer raced to the referee with blood streaming from his head and claiming a missile from the excited Ghanaian Hearts of Oak supporters had inflicted the damage. But it all backfired because a linesman had spotted the keeper cutting himself with a lump of brick. El Ouaer had done enough damage not to be able to carry on, the Tunisians had a man sent off and the Ghanaians won with a late three-goal burst.

Turning point

Tommy Hutchison was the pivotal man of the 1981 FA Cup final. He opened the scoring for Manchester City and then scored an own goal 11 minutes from time to bring Tottenham Hotspur level. Spurs won the replay 3–2.

Bruce's "spaghetti" legs ploy

A wobbly legs ploy in two European Champions League finals succeeded in winning the trophy twice for Liverpool. In 1984 Bruce Grobbelaar performed his slapstick "spaghetti" legs routine as he faced a penalty from Roma's Bruno Conti and saw the shot ballooned over the bar for Liverpool to win the penalty shoot-out. In 2006 Jerzy Dudek's homage to his predecessor produced a copycat routine in the final against Milan – and it worked again.

Unwanted double

Bert Turner scored twice in a minute to create the talking point of the 1946 FA Cup final between Derby and Charlton. After his own goal in the 85th minute he made amends by scoring at the other end to force extra time. Derby won 4–1.

Hartlepool bomb bill ignored

Hartlepool Football Club from the north-east of England sent a bill for damages to the government of defeated Germany following World War 1. The club, which has never achieved great success, had its ground bombed by German Zeppelins in 1916. The town's shipyards had been the target but, spooked by defending British fighter planes, the Zeppelin captains had turned tail for home, dropping their bombs haphazardly. One of the unfortunate recipients of several bomb hits was the club, which had its main stand, made of wood, flattened. The Germans never made good on the bill.

Target man

Fans don't seem to like Austrian goalkeeper Otto Konrad. He was hit on the head by a bottle while playing for Casino Salzburg at AC Milan, then, two years later, needed treatment for first-degree burns after being hit in the face with a flare while playing for Real Zaragoza.

Darting attack

Northern Ireland goalkeeper Pat Jennings calmly plucked a dart thrown from the crowd out of his arm during a league game for Arsenal at Nottingham Forest.

Saturday ban

Argentina's 1998 World Cup goalkeeper Carlos Roa was a member of the Seventh-day Adventist Church, which is against working on Saturdays. Roa quit football because he believed the world was about to end.

Hitting the spot

Croatian Dino Drpic ended up on the transfer list after his wife revealed that they had been "very naughty" in having made floodlit love in the centre circle of Dinamo Zagreb's Maksimir Stadium.

Meaty deal

Romanian league midfielder Ion Radu transferred from Jiul Petrosani to Valcea in 1998 in exchange for 2 tons of beef and pork. The proceeds from selling the meat paid the salaries for the other Jiul Petrosani players.

Johnston's help for a pal backfires

Winger Willie Johnston was sent home in disgrace for failing a drugs test after the first game of the 1978 World Cup finals. With fellow Scot Archie Gemmill too dehydrated to give a urine sample, Johnston stepped in – and found himself on the first plane home in shame after a farcical 3–1 defeat against Peru when a banned stimulant was found in his system. Johnston maintains he never deliberately took a performance-enhancing drug but admitted to taking a hay fever remedy. A volatile character, the Rangers winger hit the headlines again in 1980 when Aberdeen player John McMaster had to be given the kiss of life after Johnston stamped on his throat.

Tidy profit

Middlesbrough turned a huge profit when they sold Gary Pallister to Manchester United for £2.3m in 1989. Boro had given Billingham Town a set of kit, a bag of balls and a goal net for Pallister's signature in 1984.

Upkeep of the Palace hits millionaire

Some football lovers risk everything for the game and one was Mark Goldberg, who paid £23m for ownership of waning London club Crystal Palace in 1998. He was a self-made multimillionaire with expensive cars and home, but upkeep of the Palace drained it all from him. Despite the boast of bringing unprecedented success and even European football, the Premiership strugglers were relegated – along with Goldberg's finances.

Spain hit 11-goal target – exactly

As tall orders go, this was almost high-rise. In 1983 Spain needed to win by 11 clear goals to qualify for the 1984 European Championship finals. It seemed impossible even when the fall guys in the qualifying group with Holland were plucky, but untalented, Malta. Panic was beginning to set in by half-time when Malta weren't rolling over and the score was only 3–1 to Spain. Then with 30 minutes left the floodgates opened and Malta buckled for Spain to win 12–1 for an exact 11-goal margin that raised eyebrows with conspiracy theorists.

Fan anger

Relegation-threatened Guarani goalkeeper Adriano Pitarelli needed medical attention after fans stoned his car while driving home from a Brazilian league match in 1996.

Chewing it over

Sheffield United goalkeeper Paddy Kenny required 12 stitches after he had his eyebrow bitten off in a drunken brawl in a curry restaurant in 2006.

Piss-poor loser

A poor loser left a bad taste in the mouth after a provincial cup match in Italy. Knowing the victors would drink a celebration from it, a 17-year-old player with defeated team in the trophy after his team had lost in a 2009 final. Fortunately for the victorious players the offence was spotted. The presentation ceremony was cancelled and the youth who rained on the parade was suspended by his club.

Freak shot

Bayern Munich reserve goalkeeper Michael Rensing replaced first-choice Oliver Kahn because he had injured him in the warm-up. While casually firing shots at Kahn before a game against Arminia Bielefeld, Rensing accidentally bruised Kahn's eye.

Bjorge lets rip in victory

Norwegian radio commentator Bjorge Lillelien was overcome when Norway beat England 2–1 in 1981. His listeners heard: "We are the best in the world! We have beaten England 2–1 in football!! It is completely unbelievable! We have beaten England! England, birthplace of giants. Lord Nelson, Lord Beaverbrook, Sir Winston Churchill, Sir Anthony Eden, Clement Attlee, Henry Cooper, Lady Diana – we have beaten them all. Maggie Thatcher, I have a message for you in the middle of the election campaign. I have a message for you: We have knocked England out of the football World Cup. Maggie Thatcher, as they say in your language in the boxing bars around Madison Square Garden in New York: Your boys took a hell of a beating! Your boys took a hell of a beating!"

Unseasonal wishes

Sheffield Wednesday sacked Derek Dooley as manager on Christmas Eve 1973. What made the betrayal even worse was that Dooley, a prolific striker, had lost a leg playing for Wednesday 18 years before.

Lights out

Lighting and heating were among the first economies when new owners David Gold and David Sullivan took over West Ham – and its estimated £110m debts – in 2010.

Fishing for a place

England World Cup winner and angling fanatic Jack Charlton had a strange instruction method for potential fishermen. In 1984 an apprentice was so desperate to impress the then Newcastle United boss that he spent a week's wages on fishing gear and begged former defender Charlton to give him a lesson. On arrival at the riverbank, Charlton poured a bottle of famous local beer Newcastle Brown Ale in the water, dipped in the rod and within seconds was pulling out a whopper.

Mario goes back to school

Mario Balotelli has always showed he is not afraid of authority and has given many referees and managers sleepless nights with his eccentric behaviour. But in 2011 he took on the headteacher of a school as he tried to help a young Manchester City fan who was being bullied. When asked for an autograph at City's training ground by a young boy, the striker questioned why he wasn't at school. The star-struck youngster explained he was playing truant because he was being bullied. The Italian international then started a one-man crusade to help. He took the boy and his mother to the school and demanded an audience with the headteacher to make him aware of the boy's plight. Balotelli also mediated between the two boys whose dispute had led to the bullying allegations.

Jaw war

Derby County apologised to opponents Reading over the treatment of one of their injured players. Reading's Brian Howard was taunted by Derby mascot Rammie the Ram for faking injury in a December 2009 fixture. Howard had, in fact, broken his jaw.

Tackled by a jellyfish

Tough Argentinian midfielder Julio Arca was sidelined by a creature rarely found in the chilly waters of the North Sea off the north east coast of England. He was stung in 2003 by an exotic jellyfish during a Sunderland training session, broke out in a severe rash and was rushed to hospital.

Right on track

When their team coach became stranded in London traffic in 2006, Coventry City's players bought 23 single tickets for the Tube. They reached their game at Queen's Park Rangers in time and won 1–0.

Cosy club cooperation

It is rumoured that a cosy club of about 12 clubs created a cartel in an eastern European league during the 1990s to share the majority of the spoils available. Keen to stay in the league's top division, they would plot the outcome of games and even exchange home wins to ensure none of the 12 were relegated.

Millionaire raiders

Thieves used football hysteria in Brazil to stage a daring heist. After months of tunnelling 11,000 metres from a rented house in Sao Paulo to an armoured car depot, they used the end-of-season paralysis in January 2010, when everyone is glued to championship and relegation matches, to break through and steal £6m.

Banking problem

CSKA Sofia coach Luboslav Penev was barred from overseas legs of his club's 2009–10 Europa League campaign because he could not leave Bulgaria. He was involved in a dispute with a bank over a £930,000 debt claim.

Club accused of underhand antics

A Brazilian league club was accused of employing underhand tactics to disrupt their opponents in the 1990s. Under a coach who was to rise to worldwide club and international team recognition, the club was suspected of dirty tricks and their reinforcements were ball boys and the local police. The ball boys were instructed to throw, as if by mistake, extra balls on the field when the opposition was taking throw-ins and the police were encouraged to intervene in on-field fights but only use their sticks on the visiting players involved.

Mobile groan

Football trainer Dave Nicholls got a red card for using his phone on the pitch in 2005. While treating a player his phone rang, he automatically answered it and got his marching orders.

Basket ball

Goalkeeper Tom Janssens won a bet with his coach and kicked a ball into the basket of a hot-air balloon floating more than 25 metres above their training ground at Laakdal, Belgium. Two women in the basket were kind enough to throw back the ball.

Crest of a wave

With football fever still hot after South Korea reached the 2002 World Cup, head of the country's FA Chung Mong-joon made a bid for the country's presidency but withdrew at the last minute.

Beria's very long memory

Lavrenty Beria never forgot the man who humiliatingly nutmegged him in a Soviet Union lower league game in 1920. When he became the most feared man in Russia as head of the KGB, Beria was able to exact his revenge on Nikolai Starostin 19 years later. By this time Starostin had blotted his copybook again when the Spartak Moscow side he coached beat Beria's favourite club Dinamo Tbilisi in the Russian cup final. Although he was sent to the Siberian gulags for ten years on an attempted murder charge Beria had trumped up, Starostin won in the end. He returned to a hero's welcome and a coaching job with the USSR squad. Beria got a bullet in the head for war crimes.

Hooky outfit

Newcastle United's Chilean midfielder Clarence Acuna was pulled over while driving back from a club Christmas fancy dress party in England in 1999 – dressed as Captain Hook.

Club doc jailed in doping scandal

Juventus club doctor Riccardo Agricola was jailed for doping the playing squad during the 1990s. The club was said to have had enough drugs for all purposes to stock a small hospital pharmacy and Agricola was imprisoned for two years and fined €2,000 for administering banned substances.

Short celebration

Roma midfielder Daniele Di Rossi celebrated a 1–0 win over city rivals Lazio in 2009 by whipping off his shorts and running around in his underpants.

Win bonuses – from pork to porn

Football in the 21st century is not only about money where win bonuses are concerned and clubs around the world find other "currencies" to reward successful endeavour. Players at the Osasuna club in Spain received pigs in 2008, while sponsors coughed up two porn movies for squad members every time FC Copenhagen won. Iran's national squad received a Peugeot car and a cash amount for playing in the 2006 World Cup finals. When the reward is cash it can be huge: Zenit St Petersburg paid $1.6m per man for winning the 2008 UEFA Cup.

Hummer treat

Girls Aloud singer Cheryl Cole spent £14,000 in 2009 on a mini Hummer replica so that Chelsea full back hubby Ashley could drive it in the grounds of their mansion. She even added crystal monogrammed headrests and gold-plated hubcaps.

Snore draw

Striker Wayne Rooney admitted he slept through one of the most important events of his life – the draw for the 2010 World Cup finals for which England were among the favourites. Suffering sleep deprivation after the arrival of son Kai, Rooney napped as David Beckham drew a favourable group in South Africa.

Fair play pays off for Leicester

Tragedy often binds footballers and brings a new spirit of charity and so it was when Nottingham Forest midfielder Clive Clark suffered a heart attack during a league cup tie with Leicester City. The game was abandoned out of respect for the severity of the situation with Forest leading 1–0. This was remembered by sporting Leicester, managed by Gary Megson, when the game was rescheduled and the Forest goalkeeper was allowed to dribble the ball from kick-off unopposed and score the goal to restore the lead. Leicester's sportsmanship paid off – they came from behind to win 3–2.

Dopes on TV

When CCTV cameras were installed in 1985 at Notts County to curb football hooliganism, the first people arrested using the new system were two fans seen rolling a joint at the back of the terraces.

Out to grass

In the 1920s the Ipswich Town groundsman Walter Woollard kept sheep, goats and chickens at the Portman Road ground. They did their bit to crop and manure the grass and were kept below a stand.

Jammed up

A rooftop protest in London had a strange consequence – making Gillingham play in their opponent's away strip. A protester on a roof in 2008 led to the closure of a major commuter route for more then nine hours and Gillingham's kit was somewhere in the grid-locked traffic.

Figo's transfer fib provokes fury

A pig's head and a whisky bottle were thrown at Spanish international Luis Figo on his return to Barcelona's Nou Camp stadium after his controversial transfer to hated rivals Real Madrid. The fan fury in 2000 had been sparked by Figo's assertion that he would not join the Madrid club but, in an amazing about-turn, he crossed probably the most controversial soccer divide in a then world record £38.7m transfer. Barca fans set up anti-Figo websites and the player was branded "Judas" by the Catalan media. Enmity between the two clubs stems from the Spanish Civil War.

Hero worship

A teenage Dimitar Berbatov dreamt of being a star striker and even wore his Alan Shearer shirt in bed, his mother revealed. She reckoned it was a sign that her son would play in England – with Spurs and Manchester United.

Shirt sex myth

A 1992 story about disgraced British government minister David Mellor making love to his mistress wearing only the blue shirt of his beloved Chelsea was a myth. It was an embellishment invented by a PR man representing Mellor's mistress, Antonia de Sancha.

Short shrift

Irish league club Dundalk sacked defender Dave Rogers for dropping his shorts in front of fans of opponents St Patrick's Athletic. He was sent off and fired for "gross misconduct".

Royal potential

Nude model, star cricketer and exceptional Southampton footballer, C. B. Fry, was offered the throne of Albania at the height of his career early in the 20th century. He politely turned down the honour saying he couldn't afford the royal lifestyle.

Mixed up

Iranian club Esteghlal disciplined three officials in 2009 for breaking the country's laws on the sexes mixing. The club's youth team had been allowed to play their women's side.

Casanova Cassano

Sampdoria's Antonio Cassano claimed to have slept with up to 700 women in 11 years. His most fruitful period was when he was with Real Madrid from 2006 to 2008 when a friendly waiter helped smuggle girls into his hotel.

Long career

Tommy Docherty was boss of 12 clubs in a 27-year managerial career from 1961 to 1988 and even found time to manage his national team. He was famously quoted as saying he'd had "more clubs than Jack Nicklaus".

Early bath

Plymouth Argyle manager Paul Sturrock forgot he was to give a press interview before a match in 2009. He was still in his spa bath when the press arrived, so he conducted it while in the water.

Players in false passport crackdown

A crackdown on false European passports led to three South American players being banned from entering France for two years. Colombian Farid Mondragon (£30,000), Chilean Pablo Contreras (£20,000) and Argentinian Emiliano Romay (£15,000) were also fined. The 2001 prosecutions followed a crackdown over the widespread use of fake paperwork enabling players to work in the lucrative European leagues. Mondragon obtained a Greek passport to play for Metz, while Contreras' and Romay's Italian passports won them transfers to Monaco and Nice, respectively.

Tyre-ing start

Chelsea's billionaire owner Roman Abramovich got his start in business selling retread tyres in his native Russia. He moved on to perfume, tights and toothpaste – even dolls – and is now reputedly worth billions.

Battle for life

Paraguayan striker Salvador Cabanas ended up fighting for his life early in 2010 after being shot in the head by a mystery gunman. The Club America player was gunned down in a Mexico City bar.

Sepp blathers

FIFA president Sepp Blatter enraged the politically correct in 2004 when he was asked what could be done to make women's soccer more popular. His answer: "More feminine clothes like in volleyball. They could, for example, wear tighter shorts."

Romario irony

Brazil star Romario always claimed he played better for partying the night before the match. It was ironic, then, that in 1999 he was sacked by Flamengo for inappropriately partying after being knocked out of the Brazilian championship.

Name cock-up

Legendary BBC commentator Kenneth Wolstenholme refused during broadcasts to pronounce the "cock' part of Everton winger Mike Trebilcock's name. When the player scored to win the 1966 FA Cup Wolstenholme pronounced it "Trebilco".

"God's" goalie

Former Coventry City goalkeeper David Icke claimed in a 1980s TV chat-show interview that he was the "son of the godhead". A deeply religious man, he descended into crank status with his pronouncements about reptilian extraterrestrials tampering with human DNA.

Gazza and the Pope were pals

Former England and Lazio midfielder Paul Gascoigne revealed that he and Pope John Paul II used to speak on the telephone. 'His bodyguard was my bodyguard at one point. The Pope rang me up wanting to speak to me' Gazza said, 'It didn't faze me. I just said "Alreet Pope. How are you?"'

Wing play

In a scene redolent of a Harry Potter film, a Euro 2008 qualifier game in Finland was halted by the arrival of a northern eagle owl with a 2-metre wingspan. After a few crowd-silencing swoops it perched on both goals and stopped the game. Finland beat Belgium 2–0.

Chicken throw-in

Chicken literally took to the wing after Grimsby Town lost a 1996 game. It was alleged that volatile manager Brian Laws, angry at Ivano Bonetti for not trying hard enough, threw a plate of wings at the player leaving him with a fractured cheekbone.

Come again?

The Scottish accent of successful 1950s and 1960s Manchester United manager Matt Busby was said to be so strong and difficult to understand that a census taker once misheard and listed his occupation as "fruit boiler". Busby had said "footballer".

The Mrs gets in on the act

It was a totally unexpected entrance for a substitute – a furious woman brandishing an umbrella and intent on using it. The crazy moment came in 1951 when home side Spvgg Erkenschwick took the lead in a German league game with Schalke 04. In frustration, Schalke's Paul Matzkowski hammered the ball into the back of opponent Kalli Metajka but didn't reckon on the feisty Mrs Metajka, known as Friedchen, who was a spectator. Angry at the assault on her husband she marched on to the pitch, brolly in hand, and cracked Matzkowski over the head with it. He also got booked, but later made a formal apology to the Metajkas.

Giving Shev the shove

Having one of the world's most feared forwards join your squad should have been a dream – but not for Jose Mourinho of Chelsea. Andriy Shevchenko's arrival from AC Milan in 2006 in an eye-watering $45m deal didn't please the coach because in the first place he never wanted the Ukrainian international with around 250 career goals. The transfer was pushed through by Chelsea owner – and Shevchenko's friend – Roman Abramovich, and the player didn't help his situation with Mourinho by producing a series of lack-lustre performances and was selected less and less. The situation ended unhappily for both as Mourinho lost his power struggle with Abramovich and left Stamford Bridge. Shevchenko didn't improve and returned to Milan.

Injured by coffee table

In 2001 then Leeds United central defender Rio Ferdinand injured himself – doing nothing. Watching TV with his feet up on a coffee table for four hours led to a strained tendon behind his knee and several weeks on the club physio's treatment table.

On track

England defender Zat Knight was worth 30 tracksuits when he moved from non-league Rushall Olympic to Fulham in 1999. Fulham chairman Mohamed Al Fayed sent 30 tracksuits as a goodwill gesture.

Missionary zeal

Footballing Britons spread the game to other European countries during the 19th century. Austrian-based ex-pats formed First Vienna FC and the Vienna Cricket and Football Club. In Italy, Serie A's Genoa club was started by Brits as Genoa Football and Cricket Club.

Entertainment boost

A 1925 change in the English league football offside laws saw the goals per game average soar from 2.58 to 3.68. Ironically, Huddersfield Town won the First Division both sides of the radical law change.

Kitted out

Future England winger John Barnes changed clubs at 17 for a set of kit. His new club Watford made a £900,000 profit five years later when they sold him to Liverpool.

Black era

Italy's shirt colour was changed for the 1938 World Cup from its traditional azure blue to black to reflect the country's fascist regime under Mussolini. They often played to a deafening chorus of boos, chants and whistles from anti-fascist fans.

Write stuff

Zinedine Zidane left Juventus for Real Madrid in Spain in 2001 but had bumped into Real's Florentino Perez at a 1991 social event where a napkin was passed to him saying: "Do you want to play for Real Madrid?"

Jaundiced view

Conspiracy theories abounded when half the 1954 West German World Cup-winning side went down with jaundice following their surprise victory over favourites Hungary in the final. Performance-enhancing vitamin injections were hinted at as the reason half the team turned yellow.

Effing quick

The first-class soccer career of celebrity chef Gordon Ramsay lasted a total of 30 minutes. Ramsay, whose TV shows are littered with the F word, turned out for Glasgow Rangers against St Johnstone for 20 minutes and against Greenock Morton for just ten.

Cup cruise

The first World Cup tournament in 1930 in Uruguay was almost a Europe-free zone but for a late change of mind. France, Belgium and Romania decided to send squads by ship -- the only way they could afford to take part.

Scottish intransigence

Scotland refused to go to the 1950 World Cup finals even though the team were runners-up in their qualifying group. Previously the Scottish FA had decided to go only if they were group winners. England went alone to Brazil.

Bunny fun

Real Madrid's Carlos Secretario hopped to it and, in a lightning-fast move, caught a rabbit that had stopped a game against Betis at the Bernabeu during the 1996–97 season.

Putter clash

Hot-headed Welsh winger Craig Bellamy ended up labelled by the media "The Nutter with the Putter" after allegedly attacking Liverpool team-mate John Arne Riise with a golf club in 2007. The spat at a training session in Portugal cost both players two weeks' wages.

One step to a rule change

One man is credited with destroying a new offside rule implemented by England's FA in 1925. When the rules were changed that three players should be between the attacker and goal, it brought a new cavalier style to the game with a boost in goals. Uncompromising Newcastle United full back Billy McCracken soon put a stop to that. He perfected the ruse of a well-timed one step forward in order to catch many opposing forwards offside at once. His action and those of imitators led to a further change in the rules to two players between attacker and goal.

Pitch shocker

Seven players and the referee were left unconscious when lightning struck the pitch as Moroko Swallows played Jomo Cosmos in the South African Premier League in 1998. All recovered.

Fowl-er mood

Striker Robbie Fowler was left out of the Liverpool squad for the start of the 2001–02 Premiership season after kicking a ball at assistant manager Phil Thompson during training. Fowler eventually apologised but was sold to Leeds a year later.

Unbeaten

One of the holy grails of English football -- the record for going unbeaten for a whole season – took 106 years to break. Preston's "Invincibles" did it in 1898; Arsenal did not achieve it again until 2003–04.

Flute furore

Paul Gascoigne of Glasgow Rangers reopened old sectarian wounds in 1998 with a goal celebration mimicking playing the flute, a Protestant Loyalist symbol, in front of the traditionally Catholic Celtic supporters. Gazza was fined £20,000 and subjected to IRA death threats for months.

Beckham's lost boot

Manchester United lost the flying boot with which Sir Alex Ferguson famously was said to have injured David Beckham's eyebrow. The Comic Relief charity had asked if it could sell the boot as a fundraiser but were told it had got mixed up with the rest of the players' boots by mistake.

Tom Thumb yobs

The Finger Football version of Subbuteo caused a row when it came complete with thugs to recreate pitch invasions and a phrase book with sayings such as: "You're gonna get your cuticles kicked in!" The English FA said the game glorified criminals, but makers Flair insisted it was intended as fun.

Take a break

The first replacement in the 1994 World Cup match between Bulgaria and Mexico was not a player. A broken crossbar had to be substituted at the Giants Stadium in New Jersey.

White horse wins by a nose

Bosses of the new Wembley Stadium had plenty of choices for a name for the bridge that thousands of fans use whenever there is a game at the football showpiece. On the list was World Cup-winning manager Sir Alf Ramsey; the massive fundraising organisation Live Aid; star players Sir Bobby Charlton and Bobby Moore – even Jim Baxter, Scotland's most accomplished player who had died relatively young. The winner was White Horse Bridge after Billy the police horse, which potentially saved many lives when the crush of fans for the first Wembley final in 1923 threatened to get out of hand.

Kev's got a point

Sunderland striker Kevin Phillips gave traffic cops a laugh when they stopped him for speeding in 2002. When told his punishment would include three points on his licence, and with Sunderland going through a rough patch, he replied: "Any chance of giving them to the team?"

Costly laughs

Chile's under-20 football squad were fined in 2002 – for laughing. The extraordinary decision was taken by the country's FA following an incident at the junior football tournament in Uruguay. Midfielder Luis Jara said: "Someone told a joke and we all laughed really hard, but the coach was not happy."

Toy menace

Kidderminster captain Sean Flynn missed an English Third Division league match after tripping over his son's toy car and falling downstairs. The midfielder was knocked out and needed stitches in a lip wound.

Player's second City tour

Given the depth of hostile feelings between them, Birmingham's three football clubs have always been reluctant to take each other's players, especially locally born ones with special affiliations. The exception was Robert Hopkins who played not only for his beloved Birmingham City, but also for local rivals Aston Villa and West Bromwich Albion between 1979 and 1989. It was said that while playing for Aston Villa for four years, he kept a Birmingham City badge pinned under the Villa one and ultimately got his dream move there. He later left for West Bromwich, but returned to Birmingham City to finish his career.

Spoil sport

Revered Italian star Roberto Baggio was tackled by an over-zealous beach attendant. Baggio was showing off his skills to holiday-makers on a beach in Italy's Liguria region when the ball was snatched from him and he was told football was not allowed.

Well done, sport

A small-town football team in England secured a sponsorship deal with Australian Aborigines in 2002. A fan of Clitheroe FC of the North-West Counties League, Bruce Dowles, persuaded the Aboriginal and Torres Strait Islander Commission to sponsor a match, paying £125 for the ball and a programme advert.

Bone of contention

Brazilian star Ze Roberto was reportedly excited by his Bundesliga debut for Bayern Munich in 2002. A photograph showed midfielder Ze Roberto in an apparent state of arousal but the player claimed it was his new padded shorts.

Women off the menu

Greek national team manager Otto Rehhagel noticed his players becoming distracted by the waitresses in a Romanian hotel and had them replaced by men. It worked to focus the Greeks on a tricky away match and they beat Romania 1–0.

Superfan

Eighty-year-old Norman Windram claimed in 2002 to have watched every single Manchester United home game since 1926. At four years old he saw his first match and had clocked up roughly 1,800 games.

Sitting with the enemy

Ron Atkinson didn't know his way about the Nottingham Forest ground at his first match as manager. Mistakenly, he sat in the dugout of visitors Arsenal and fans couldn't make him aware of the error. He only realised when he saw Dutch ace Dennis Bergkamp and reportedly quipped: "We haven't got him, have we?"

Stamping his authority

Much-travelled Norwegian striker Tore Andre Flo was immortalised in his country on a postage stamp. His scoring of the winning goal against Brazil in the 1998 World Cup finals was chosen as the best moment in Norwegian football history.

Heads you lose

Meeting the mighty Brazil is every international player's dream and no less so for Rajko Mitic of Yugoslavia at the 1950 World Cup finals. As he bounded excitedly from the dressing room he hit his forehead on a girder, severely cutting it. Without Mitic for the first 20 minutes, Yugoslavia lost 2–0 and were eliminated.

Lined up

When linesman Dennis Drewitt pulled a calf muscle at an Arsenal–Liverpool game in 1972 the call went out for a qualified referee in the crowd. Up stepped BBC TV pundit Jimmy Hill from the stands and, donning an ill-fitting tracksuit, he proceeded to run the line to playful barracking from spectators.

Wee doggy

England goal king Jimmy Greaves had a dampener on his appearance in the England–Brazil match in the 1962 World Cup in Chile. He managed to capture a small dog that had invaded the pitch, but the terrified pooch pee-ed on Greavsie's England jersey. Brazil winger Garrincha thought the incident so funny he adopted the dog.

Sense of humour failure

Pedantic referee Dougie Smith didn't see the funny side of cheeky-chappy Paul Gascoigne. Having dropped his yellow cards on the pitch when refereeing a 1995 Rangers–Hibernian Scottish league match, Gazza helped pick them up, then brandishing a card, playfully "booked" the ref. Smith retaliated with a real booking.

Knockout drops

During the rough and tumble of a full-bloodied 1930 World Cup semi-final between Argentina and the USA, the Americans' trainer raced on to the field to remonstrate with the referee. He threw his medical bag to the ground, cracked open a bottle of chloroform and knocked himself out.

Unfair trip?

Spartak Moscow captain Radoslav Kovac was booked for tackling a fan from behind. With his side trailing 2–1 to rivals Lokomotiv in a 2007 Russian league match, proceedings were interrupted by a shirtless fan on the pitch. Kovac tackled the unwanted visitor with a perfectly executed "playground" trip – and picked up a yellow card.

Ring wrong

Swiss league Paolo Diogo was so overjoyed at scoring a rare goal for Geneva against Schaffhausen in 2004 that he hurdled the perimeter fence to celebrate with fans. His wedding ring caught on the fence and ripped the top off his finger. The referee added a yellow card.

Sorry, mate

Prodding his best friend with his foot got Deportivo Coruna's Jorge Andrade sent off. When friend and former Porto team-mate Deco was fouled and stayed down, Andrade's gentle kick to stop Deco's play-acting was spotted by the ref who saw it as violent conduct.

Club says sorry with free passes

Frustrated fans of Weymouth Town were given free entry to a match to make up for a previous week's debacle. Weymouth, bottom of the Blue Square Conference South league in February 2010, brought their appalling run of form to a head with a 0–6 home thrashing by Basingstoke Town. Embarrassed Weymouth chairman George Rolls immediately issued an apology and offered loyal fans free entry to the next home match against second-placed Braintree Town. Weymouth's inept defending gave Basingstoke striker Mitchell Bryant the chance to break the Conference record by scoring all six goals.

Red mist ref

Spanish referee Jose Manuel Barro Escandon went red-card crazy when a regional first division match between Recreativo Linense and Saladillo de Algeciras descended into a mass brawl. After abandoning the game he went into the dressing rooms and dished out nine red cards per side.